GW00481119

APHRODISIA

APHRODISIA

HOMEMADE POTIONS TO MAKE LOVE MORE LIKELY, MORE PLEASURABLE, AND MORE POSSIBLE

JULIE BRUTON-SEAL AND MATTHEW SEAL

LYONS PRESS
GUILFORD, CONNECTICUT
An imprint of Globe Pequot Press

To buy books in quantity for corporate use
or incentives, call **(800) 962-0973**
or e-mail **premiums@GlobePequot.com**.

First published in Great Britain by Merlin Unwin Books Ltd., 2012
First Lyons Press edition, 2012
Copyright © 2012 Julie Bruton-Seal and Matthew Seal

Lyons Press is an imprint of Globe Pequot Press.

Text design: Maggie Peterson
Layout artist: Maggie Peterson
Project editor: Kristen Mellitt
All photographs by Julie Bruton-Seal unless otherwise noted.

Library of Congress Cataloging-in-Publication Data is available on file.

ISBN 978-0-7627-7987-1

Printed in the United States of America

10 9 8 7 6 5 4 3 2 1

Please note:
The information in *Aphrodisia* is not intended to replace the advice and care of
a qualified medical practitioner. Heed the cautions given, and if already taking
prescribed medicines or if you are pregnant, seek professional advice before using
herbal aphrodisiacs.

CONTENTS

Know that these things favour coition: health, freedom from worry, absence of preoccupation, a cheerful disposition, a generous diet, wealth, and variety in the features and complexion of the woman.

—*Sheikh Nefwazi*, The Perfumed Garden *(written 1420s)*

INTRODUCTION

1.   What are aphrodisiacs?

If you look the word up, aphrodisiacs are said to arouse or intensify sexual desire. This refers to Aphrodite, the Greek goddess of love in all its forms. There is a hint of "love potions," something to make us fall in love. The goddess is patron of many plants and other products that help us in our search.

Anthurium: aphrodisiac by "signature" but not in practice

The notion of aphrodisiacs includes our mental and emotional response as well as the physical pleasure of sex. So the term is spacious enough to bring in desire, love and romance, mood and setting, libido and placebo.

Almost everything we eat has been considered aphrodisiac at some time in history. Anything new and exotic or expensive acquires a hint of the erotic—look at potatoes and tomatoes in Elizabethan Europe or maca today.

2.   Do aphrodisiacs work?

If you go down the scientific route, you will note a paucity of human clinical trials for even the most ancient of aphrodisiacs and conclude that there is little proof that they work at all. If you go a more "ethnobotanical" route, you'll take into account the continued use in traditional societies of many aphrodisiacs, whether by shamans or by society in general. If these plants don't work, why on earth would they continue to be used for thousands of years?

If it's all delusion and placebo, here's a thought: The word placebo itself means "I shall please." Placebo is powerful, occurring both in scientific method and in issues of belief and conviction. Write off placebo, and you discard an entire mental/emotional aspect of how healing and loving alike are manifested.

This leads to the ancient idea of the doctrine of signatures. The way things looked was considered to give clues to how they could be used. In the case of aphrodisiacs, something that looks erotic can be arousing even if it lacks all aphrodisiac action. Hence the ancient and still persistent trade in rhino horns, tiger penises, bear paws, deer musk, and so on that is driving animals to extinction. For the record, we do not accept these products as aphrodisiacs, and they have no place in this book.

3.   How do aphrodisiacs work?

The actions of aphrodisiacs are subtle and multileveled. Many are **stimulants**—these may be hot plants, like chili or pepper, which heat up the body and stimulate metabolism, boosting circulation and body secretions. Other stimulants such as coffee and cola work on our nervous system.

Ginkgo is often included in aphrodisiac formulas for its circulation-enhancing properties. This particular tree also has breastlike growth on the branches, making it suggestive as well.

The **fragrant aphrodisiacs,** like rose, jasmine, and ylang-ylang, also work via the nervous system. Smells have a powerful effect on our emotions. We all know how a scent from long ago can take us back in an instant. Fragrances help arouse all our senses. Combined with touch in the form of massage with scented oils, they can be even more powerful.

Many of the aphrodisiacs we chose for this book are **rejuvenating tonics,** restoratives, or *rasayana* herbs. Sexuality sits at the peak of good health and vitality, so libido, or sex drive, is often the first thing to go if we are tired or ill. These vitality-restoring herbs are particularly helpful for anyone who is depleted, tired from working too hard, or under long-term stress of any kind. Parents of young children may be young themselves but could really benefit from these herbs. We also tend to need them more as we get older.

Then there are herbs that work directly on our hormone levels to **increase libido,** such as tribulus and shatavari. These are particularly useful during andropause (or male menopause) and menopause, when levels of sexual hormones drop in men and women.

Last but not least are the **relaxing aphrodisiacs,** which go hand in hand with the restoratives. Often all we need is a little help to relax and unwind, letting go of the worries and preoccupations of the day. This may be a glass of red wine, some nutmeg, a shot of kava kava, or an aphrodisiac.

Many of the plants we chose for this book **improve sexual performance**, more obviously an issue for men. Many increase blood flow to the genitals, which helps with arousal in both sexes. The whole issue of erectile dysfunction (ED) needs addressing, if sales of Viagra and similar pills are anything to go by.

Clitoria: a wild, twining vine from southern India, but not an aphrodisiac, despite its name and appearance

Medication, such as high blood pressure drugs, can cause difficulties in this area, as can diabetes and other illnesses. And of course stress is a serious hindrance to good sex. Lack of desire in men is itself the cause of stress and embarrassment, and many of our aphrodisiac herbs can help. Men are notoriously unwilling to discuss these issues, but the idea of making their own aphrodisiacs may tempt them. Many of the herbs we discuss improve fertility in women and increase quality and volume of sperm in men.

4.   Which are the best aphrodisiacs?

How did we compile our list? First, we looked at aphrodisiac traditions across the world, especially in India and China. Traditional Chinese medicine texts go back some two thousand years, and aphrodisiacs, like ginseng and horny goat weed, were important then, as they remain today. Ayurvedic tradition in India is older still, with one of its eight disciplines being *Vajikarna*, the study of aphrodisiacs. Classic Ayurvedic herbs like ashwagandha, shatavari, and ginger are used by herbalists East and West and well deserve their inclusion here.

Chocolate, maca, and chili are from the New World, yohimbe and cola from Africa—each of them traditional aphrodisiacs and central to local culture, and now available everywhere.

Western traditions come in, too, as in roses given to the beloved on Valentine's Day since at least Chaucer's time (he died in 1400). He wrote of the rose: *"for this was sent on Saint Valentyne's day, / when every foul cometh to choose his mate."*

Some plants are included here because we discovered their benefits ourselves years ago, like cnidium. Others are from perfumery, like jasmine, ylang-ylang, and the products of the orange tree. In all, we have evolved a list of our own favorite aphrodisiacs that are effective; are either food, medicine, or perfume; are sustainable; have no or few side effects or toxicity (yohimbe is an exception); and that we confidently recommend to you.

Many aphrodisiac books list animals, birds, fish, and other nonplant aphrodisiacs. This book doesn't. We draw our personal ethical line at taking animal life for human pleasure.

We have attempted to describe in either our main or secondary lists all these most popular plant aphrodisiacs, and others that came lower down in our ranking. It's no more than a snapshot, but we hope a useful one.

5.   Why make your own aphrodisiacs?

There are many good reasons. We know you can buy many of the herbs we list in pill or capsule form, and that they work, but taking a pill isn't very sexy. Wouldn't you rather make a wonderful dessert laced with ginseng that is beautiful and excites the taste buds? Or create a massage oil that transports you into another world, awakening sensuality and pleasure? Pills and capsules (and penis pumps) are just so clinical.

Another factor is that if you buy a quality dried herb from an herbalist or reputable supplier, you'll know what you're getting. You can smell it and taste it, and have the fun of thinking of creative ways to use it.

There is no quality control on aphrodisiac products sold on the Internet, and with a pill or a capsule it's hard to be sure. Expensive herbs are often substituted with cheaper ones, and sometimes pharmaceutical drugs are included in products claiming to be natural. Make your own aphrodisiacs from good ingredients, and you will be more than a passive, ill-informed buyer.

Making your own is also far cheaper, which is always helpful—we're sure you can think of something pleasurable to do with the money you save.

6.   Is Viagra an aphrodisiac?

Viagra, Cialis, Levitra, and their rivals are erection aids for men, not aphrodisiacs as such. This is not to say they don't have their uses and their followers. Since 1998, when Viagra was launched, upwards of a billion diamond-shaped blue pills have been bought, and nearly 30 million men have used them. Within months Viagra became the most purchased drug ever.

These drugs are known as PDE-5 inhibitors, which work by relaxing the blood vessels in the penis, allowing blood to flood into it and cause a prolonged erection, even in men with seemingly permanent ED. Aside from the dollar price are the unpleasant side effects of upset stomach, headaches, and flushing, with greater risks for men with either high or low blood pressure. There were a number of early fatalities with Viagra, now much reduced by tightening up the prescription conditions for doctors. There is little or no control on knockoff lookalikes sold online, or as yet on advertising claims. It's not surprising that Viagra is the most counterfeited drug in history.

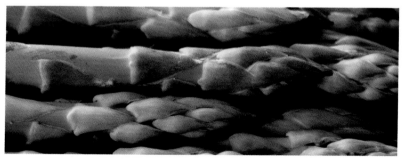

Asparagus spears: They look the part, and many eaters find they are.

But, to be evenhanded, Viagra has restored sexual life to men who had previously given up on it. Its very notoriety has helped people talk more freely about sexual problems, a revolution apparent in the shift in male terminology from "impotence" to "sexual dysfunction." The equivalent female code-switch has been from "frigidity" to "loss of libido," and surely this is welcome progress.

7. Is alcohol an aphrodisiac?

A friend of ours says a glass of good red does it for her. Champagne drunk from a stripper's stilettos used to do it in Paris, we are led to believe. A glass or a pint sets up any beer drinker, but the reality is that hops in beer are estrogenic and act as an anaphrodisiac for men. While a little beer is sexually stimulating and a man thinks he is irresistible, a lot proves he is not—"brewer's droop" is an apt name. But men may not suffer performance anxiety after overindulgence in beer because they're more likely to be asleep.

As we discuss for nutmeg and mace, the effect of alcohol is dose dependent, so we say alcohol is aphrodisiacal up to a point. That tipping point differs for each individual, and some people spend a lifetime enjoying the search for it.

What we call "Dutch courage" is nothing new. Chaucer again, on a bridegroom: "*He drinkyth ipocras, claret and vernage, / Of spyces hot, t'encreasen his courage.*" Hippocras was a medieval favorite, a blend of warming spices and wine; even before then "honeymoons" went better with the honey drink mead. Tinctures of herbs in alcohol remain part of the herbalist's armory, and we include several in our recipes.

8. Are aphrodisiacs the same for men and women?

Technically some aphrodisiacs are "women's herbs," like shatavari, and some are "men's herbs," like ginseng and yohimbe. But many are adaptogens, and most herbs are wise, so in practice we suggest you freely try any and every recipe we give and see what it does for you.

There needn't be a battle of the sexes over aphrodisiacs, but we do need to understand each other. Comedian Billy Crystal teases: "*Women need a reason to have sex, men just need a place.*" And comic writer Kathy Lette: "*For centuries men have wondered what a woman really wants in bed. I'll tell you: breakfast!"* Let's be nice to each other. We are in this thing together, stress and all, aging and all. Any day is a possible Valentine's; any meal can be a love meal. If our loving is fulfilling, maybe we won't need aphrodisiacs anyway.

9. Are aphrodisiacs dangerous?

The writer Ovid was as much in favor of aphrodisiacs as the next wealthy Roman of two thousand years ago, but he did warn about *philters* (love potions), *which disturb the balance of the mind and illumine the fires of furious madness.* Aphrodisiacs have always had a dark side, perhaps deriving from Aphrodite herself: One of her identities was Aphrodite Porne, the patron of prostitutes and love for sale, whose name is still recalled in pornography.

The deadly link of aphrodisiac and poison—passion and toxicity—has a long folk memory. The emperor Caligula's wife and, later, Catherine de Medici and Lucrezia Borgia, are only some of history's poisoners who beguiled their victims with fatal potions disguised in alcohol or sumptuous aphrodisiac foods. The modern equivalent is the "date-rape" drug Rohypnol.

Special delivery breakfast: hot croissants and herb butter with spiced coffee

We appreciate that the idea of danger can be a turn-on in itself. We all know about the "aphrodisiac of power" or "aphrodisiac of money." It's about influence and control as well as risk and danger.

We accept that, but we draw the line at poisons. Our notion of aphrodisiacs is far removed from the Marquis de Sade's in lacing chocolates with the deadly cantharides (the terrible Spanish fly) and watching several prostitutes suffer in agony—he was jailed for this stunt but not executed. Aphrodisiacs should not be something you put into somebody's food or drink without their knowledge and for selfish ends. Can't aphrodisiacs be shared in full awareness and informed consent in our own private time?

10. Where do I get aphrodisiacs?

Sex shops don't sell aphrodisiacs as a rule, and doctors and pharmacists don't often prescribe them, so where do you find them? This book recommends you make your own, as appealing foods or drinks rather than as pills bought online. Some plants, like roses or jasmine, can be grown at home, but most need to be sourced as raw materials. For the more exotic plants, check the suppliers listed in "Resources."

An herbalist will provide quality herbs as well as give you advice. Find an

Pomegranate: ancient symbol of Aphrodite and modern aphrodisiac

herbalist in the Yellow Pages, at your health store or complementary therapy clinic, or via the professional associations listed in "Resources."

Most purchasing of aphrodisiacs has been on-line, in an as yet unregulated marketplace. Along with sites offering Viagra and like products, thousands tout "herbal aphrodisiacs." Some sites have good information, but most don't, not even listing ingredients or risks. We advise you not to entrust such sites with your money and health.

Finally, don't rush it; give these plants time. In Mae West's words: *"Anything worth doing is worth doing slowly."*

PART I

MAKE YOUR OWN APHRODISIACS

ASHWAGANDHA

Ashwagandha is one of the most important tonics and aphrodisiacs in Ayurveda, the age-old medical system of India. It promotes sexual potency and sperm production.

Ashwagandha, *Withania somnifera,* is a smallish shrub in the nightshade family whose root is the medicinal part. It is native to India and Africa.

It is also called winter cherry and Indian ginseng.

It's generally very safe, although it's not recommended for use during pregnancy or for people on sedatives or allergic to nightshade family species. There are minimal side effects, with no recorded drug interactions.

● calming
● tonic
● adaptogen

Ashwagandha is a key herb in Ayurveda, India's "science of life." In Western terms ashwagandha is an adaptogen (a class of plants that helps a person adapt to stress and build overall immunity), as ginseng is. Indeed, ashwagandha is sometimes called "the Indian ginseng," although the two plants are not botanically related. It is as central to the Indian culture of health as ginseng is to China's.

Ashwagandha is equally diverse in its benefits, used to treat exhaustion, loss of muscle tone, nervous disorders, depression, and anxiety; it's high in usable iron, so it is good for anemia, and it is also a sedative (as its Latin name, *somnifera,* suggests). In Ayurveda, the herb is known as a *rasayana*, a rejuvenating plant that strengthens the life force and helps people recover zest for living. It is helpful to the old and to the young, and is a supporting presence for those recuperating from illness.

Above all in India, ashwagandha is seen as a superb reproductive tonic for both sexes and is the country's most powerful and popular aphrodisiac.

While there is as yet little clinical evidence in the West to substantiate this use, as a sympathetic American ethnobotanist notes, three thousand years and millions of satisfied patients is its own evidence. Why, he asks, conduct a study to determine if people get wet when they take showers?

There can be little doubt that ashwagandha is an effective, safe, and reliable aphrodisiac. It is far more than a sex aid—the beautiful thing about *rasayanas* and adaptogens is that they treat people rather than symptoms, invigorating the body, mind, and psyche, bringing them into harmony.

As many stressed people know too well, loss of libido spirals down along with loss of self-esteem, fatigue, and lack of interest in sex or much of anything else. Ashwagandha is able to reverse the negative spiral and restore strength and

a healthy libido—in short, sexual wellness—for both sexes, young or old. The central idea of vigor is captured in its Hindi name, which translates as "strength of a horse"—a more generous and understanding version than the disparaging alternative sometimes seen in Western texts: "smell of horse urine."

The benefits of ashwagandha are most apparent if it is used regularly over a long period. It restores stressed adrenals and strengthens the whole body.

The powder is easy to incorporate into food. An herbalist friend has some in her oatmeal every morning, and it can be added to soups and smoothies. Do taste the powder before you add it to recipes, however, as it has a slight bitterness that does not go well with everything. We'd suggest starting with a smaller amount and building up as you get used to the flavor. Traditional preparations often include milk and ghee (clarified butter).

For massage, ashwagandha can be infused with sesame oil as a carrier. This creates a beautiful earthy oil, which, because ashwagandha is an adaptogen, can be deeply relaxing or stimulating, depending on circumstances.

Ashwagandha Tincture

It is easy to make your own tinctures. Fill a jar with the herb (here, ashwagandha root), then pour in vodka to cover it. Put the lid on and shake to remove bubbles, topping off if necessary. Keep in a cupboard for a month or so, shaking every few days. Strain and bottle. Take from 1 to 3 teaspoons daily.

Evening Energizing Cocoa

Ashwagandha root is traditionally boiled in milk as a beverage. We like to combine it with cocoa to make an energizing and restorative evening drink. For each mug of milk or almond milk, use ½ to 1 teaspoon ashwagandha powder, 2 teaspoons cocoa powder (or to taste), and ¼ teaspoon cardamom powder. Bring just to a boil, then remove from heat. Add a little vanilla extract and sweeten with honey or maple syrup.

CARDAMOM

Cardamom is a tasty way to spice up your love life. It has a wonderful flavor that will complement both sweet and savory dishes, and it has an ancient reputation as a warming and invigorating aphrodisiac.

Elletaria cardamomum, or Elachi, is a tropical plant in the ginger family, native to south India. It is the seed pod and seeds that are used as a spice.

Unusually, the pretty white flowers and green seed pods emerge from the plant's rhizomes.

It is safe for children and the elderly, with no known interactions or toxicity.

● mild stimulant

Cardamom is an ancient aromatic oil-yielding plant that in its native south India is known as "queen of spices" (pepper is "king"). It was and is chewed as a favorite digestive and palate cleanser, and as the go-to spice for all matters alimentary, from bad breath to diarrhea. But an aphrodisiac?

It has long been regarded as such in Ayurvedic and Middle Eastern traditions. Modern research identifies one component of ripe cardamom seeds as *1,8 cineole*. This compound is a central nervous system stimulant (in Indian terms, it gives "digestive fire"), which also helps impart the attractive eucalyptus note to the aroma.

In Ayurveda, cardamom is believed to increase sexual potency and, when added to coffee in the Middle East, is either a drink to welcome guests or a mood setter for lovers once guests have gone. We have found that adding cardamom takes the "jitteriness" out of coffee, and we grind up pods with the coffee beans, or make a masala chai with crushed cardamom seeds and other aromatics.

Cardamom is a warming and piquant addition to cakes, syrups, and ice creams, and works well for savory meals such as curries and rice. The best pods are lime green in color and free from any tears in the outer husk, with black seeds.

CHAI FOR LOVERS

Grate a piece of **fresh ginger** about 1 inch long into a saucepan. Add 2 cups **water**; 3 cardamom pods, crushed; 5 **black peppercorns**; a piece of **cinnamon stick**; and 2 or 3 **cloves**.

Heat and simmer for 10 minutes.

Add ½ cup **milk** and a rounded teaspoon of **tea**; simmer 10 minutes more. Strain. If you like, sprinkle a little **nutmeg** on top and add a few drops of **vanilla extract**. Sweeten with **honey**.

Refreshing and satisfying, especially after lovemaking.

CARDAMOM SYRUP

This syrup is delicious on fruit salads, or simply poured over ripe mango. Crush 2 tablespoons of **cardamom pods**. Put in a saucepan with 2 cups **water** and simmer gently with the lid on for about half an hour.

Strain out the cardamom and return liquid to the pan. Add 1 cup **sugar** and bring to a boil, boiling until reduced by about half and the syrup begins to thicken. Add the juice of **half a lemon**, bring to a boil again, then remove from the heat. Bottle.

CARDAMOM & CINNAMON COCKTAIL

Make **cardamom syrup** as above. Follow same process to make a **cinnamon syrup**, using a 4-inch **cinnamon stick**. Put equal amounts of the syrups in a glass, so that about one quarter of the glass is filled. Top up the glass with **soda water**, add **ice**, and top with a pinch of **nutmeg** or **cola nut powder** (optional). As a variation, use a smaller glass and make it an alcoholic drink with a shot of your favorite liquor.

CHILI

If you really want to heat up your love life, chilis are the obvious choice. They increase blood flow and will help other aphrodisiacs get to where they're needed.

Sweet and chili peppers are both Capsicum species in the nightshade (Solanaceae) family. Native to Central America, they grow best under hot conditions.

Good for the heart and circulation, chilis are beneficial to mucous membranes and to stop bleeding.

If you are a "hot" person, chilis may not be a good choice.

Take care when handling very hot chilis—don't rub your eyes or get chili on any delicate skin areas.

● stimulant

Chili is the hottest of hot herbs, with its very own heat-measuring scale, called Scoville Units (SU). Sweet peppers score 0 to 100 SU, cayenne and Tabasco 30,000 to 50,000 SU. Habanero, at 100,000 to 300,000 SU, is not even the hottest.

Clearly it pays to know your peppers: A chili "high" is one thing, but take the wrong strength chili for your constitution or state of health, and you can incur unbearable pain from mouth to anus.

The active ingredient in chili is capsaicin, whose effect is to open up cell membranes, triggering a pain mechanism that rapidly passes to other cells. But capsaicins are not just pain transmitters; they also open the blood vessels, easing the flow to peripheral organs, the hands or feet, and genital areas. This is why chilis are good for rheumatism, lumbago, or arthritis, including being rubbed on externally, and why they help prevent clogging of arteries (atherosclerosis) and burn body fat, making them good in weight-loss diets.

Promoting better blood circulation is good news for aphrodisiac users, especially those with joint pain. Add in chili's benefits for heart health (they also reduce LDL, or "bad" cholesterol, and equalize blood pressure), more vitamin C than citrus, and the capacity to kill pathogens in the body, and you need to thank Christopher Columbus (who looked for India and pepper but found the Americas and chili)!

STUFFED CHILI PEPPERS

Slice large **chilis** in half lengthwise. (You can use long sweet peppers if chili is too hot for you.) Remove the seeds. Sprinkle a few **pine nuts** into each, then fill with crumbled **cheese** and sprinkle with chopped **dill leaf.**

Bake in the oven at about 350°F until the cheese has melted and is beginning to brown. Serve hot.

FRESH HOT SAUCE

This sauce can be served to liven up any occasion and is delicious as an accompaniment to a variety of dishes. You can adjust the proportions to suit your taste buds. It will keep in the refrigerator for several days.

Take a few fresh red or green **chilis,** some cloves of **garlic,** and a few chunks of fresh **ginger.** Put in a blender or food processor, adding enough **extra virgin olive oil** to blend into a paste.

HINT FOR HOT CHILI MOUTH
Capsaicin is not water soluble, so water will not cool chili heat; indeed, it might spread it. Use alcohol, yogurt, or milk instead. Avoid the seeds, which have the most capsaicin.

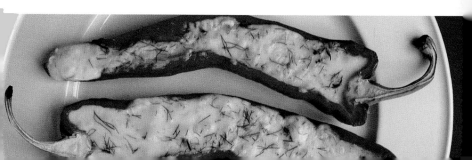

CHOCOLATE

Chocolate: the world's favorite and universal aphrodisiac. Called "the food of the gods," it is given on Valentine's Day as a symbol of love and in the form of Easter eggs for fertility. But have you thought why it works so well?

Chocolate was originally taken as a bitter drink. In the pre-Columbian civilizations of South and Central America, the beans were so valuable they were used as currency: money growing on trees.

Montezuma, the Aztec king, was reported to drink 50 cups of a specially prepared foamy drink called Xocolatl every day from a golden goblet. This drink, made from cocoa beans with vanilla and chilis, reputedly gave him the strength and virility to keep the royal ladies happy.

Eating chocolate makes us feel happier, and not just because it tastes so good. One intriguing reason is that it melts at the same temperature as human body heat (93–100°F), giving it the special quality chocolatiers call "mouthfeel."

Chocolate has small amounts of the chemical phenylethylamine (PEA), which is a mild mood elevator. This is the chemical our brain produces in response to feelings of joy and love. Eating chocolate triggers these same feelings.

Theobroma cacao, the cocoa or cacao tree, is a small tropical tree native to Mexico and Central America.

It is the seed (or bean) of the rugby ball–size fruit that is used to make chocolate.

Dark chocolate has been shown to be good for the heart.

- euphoric
- stimulant

Chocolate's main alkaloid is theobromine, a heart stimulant. Chocolate also boosts serotonin levels. Serotonin is a neurotransmitter produced by the body, which acts as our brain's own antidepressant—another way that chocolate makes us feel good.

Further, chocolate acts to lift endorphin levels in the brain. Endorphins are what flood the brain during times of peak physical exertion, creating the sensation of a permeating bliss, such as the "runner's high."

Dark chocolate and cocoa contain high levels of flavonoids, which act as powerful antioxidants in the body, mopping up free radicals and slowing our aging. Recent research shows how flavonoids encourage vascular-wall health and the functioning of blood vessels, both significant for overall as well as sexual health.

These positive health effects are most pronounced in chocolates that are high in cocoa and low in added sugar. We unashamedly recommend taking the elitist route, so forget mass market versions and go for quality. This is an affair of the heart!

The raw cocoa pod contains about 50 brown beans. The surrounding white pulp is sweet.

Chocolate Spice Cake

Sift into a large bowl:

> 3 cups **unbleached all-purpose flour**
>
> ½ cup **cocoa** powder
>
> 2 cups **sugar**
>
> 2 teaspoons **baking soda**
>
> 1 teaspoon **salt**

Add: 2 cups **water** or **cold coffee**

> 2 tablespoons cider **vinegar**
>
> 2 teaspoons **vanilla extract**
>
> ½ teaspoon each **cinnamon** and **cardamom powder**
>
> ½ cup plus 2 tablespoons **vegetable oil** (olive, sunflower, etc.)

Stir well and pour into two greased and floured 8-inch cake pans, or one larger heart-shaped pan and the rest into a cupcake pan that yields 8–10 cupcakes.

Bake in a preheated oven at 350°F for 30 minutes for the 8-inch pans. Cupcakes will cook in about 15 minutes, and larger pans may take up to an hour—test with a straw to see if they are done.

Cool on a cake rack, then remove from pan. Layer with **whipped cream** flavored with **vanilla** and a pinch of **cinnamon,** or cover with ganache (recipe below).

Chocolate Ganache

Ganache is simply chocolate and cream mixed together. The basic recipe uses roughly equal weights of chocolate and cream, but the proportions can be varied according to taste.

Bring 1.75 oz. **heavy cream** just to a boil and stir in 1.75 oz. of either grated or melted **dark chocolate**. Pour over cakes, dip fruit in it, or let it set and use a melon baller to scoop out balls to roll in cocoa powder as truffles.

CNIDIUM

Cnidium looks like a typical member of the carrot family, with the usual white umbrella of small blossoms. The seeds are small, flat, and light brown.

Cnidium seed is a Chinese aphrodisiac that can be eaten raw to great effect. *Cnidium monnieri* or *She chuang zi* is a Chinese member of the carrot family (Apiaceae).

Use the dried seeds. Also useful for skin problems.

- stimulant
- increases libido
- improves performance

At first glance, the cnidium is nothing spectacular, but please taste the seeds: A pinch begins as bland, if nutty, and turns into something like celery seed and then dill. The taste gradually grows warmer, more tingling and numbing, leaving the mouth and whole digestive system awakened. The effect goes deeper still to the sexual organs, working quite quickly, and it lasts for hours.

This is a traditional Chinese aphrodisiac, *She chuang zi* or snake bed plant, that is not much known in the West. More Internet aphrodisiac formulas now use it (often with dodder and schisandra), and we rate it highly.

Others share this view: In a random test of several aphrodisiacs on half a dozen friends, all put cnidium over yohimbe, a much more reputed herbal aphrodisiac. Both males and females reported a definite rapid increase in libido and energy.

Cnidium is also used externally (the seeds are ground up in water) in China as an intimate wash; it is effective, too, in this form for treating eczema and ringworm.

We find taking cnidium is simplicity itself: Just chew or swallow a teaspoonful of the seeds, which you can buy from your herbalist or in an Asian health store. Try grinding the seeds and sprinkle on food as a condiment, for soups or stews, or in a salad dressing. But as the raw seed is so good, why bother with other versions?

COLA NUT

Cola nut will be most familiar for its use in soft drinks bearing its name, but it has valuable stimulant, tonic, and aphrodisiac effects. It has the ability to stimulate and strengthen at the same time.

Cola (or kola) is known as a "nut" but is the seed of a large West African forest tree. The nut has been chewed as a stimulant, digestive, and aphrodisiac in western and central Africa for thousands of years, and its use was central to traditional life-cycle celebrations. In Hausa society, for example, a bride's mouth was touched with cola on her wedding night.

Cola nut, used either dried or fresh, contains three stimulants: theobromine (as in chocolate), caffeine (as in coffee), and kolanin. Its level of caffeine is higher than that of coffee (about 3 percent vs. 2

Cola flowers

Cola, kola, goora, or guru nut; *Cola nitida, C. acuminata,* Sterculiaceae family

Cola comes from a large tropical tree native to West Africa, now also grown in tropical South America. It produces creamy white flowers with red centers, followed by pods containing fleshy white or red seeds (the "nuts").

Use the powder or tincture.

Also medicinal for diarrhea and dysentery, asthma, and bronchitis.

● stimulant

Avoid in pregnancy and in cases of hypertension, but it is generally safe in moderate quantities. No reports of toxicity or drug interaction problems.

percent), and cola is sweetly astringent, which made it an excellent ingredient for the newly developed Coca-Cola in 1886 and Pepsi-Cola in 1893. Most of the cola crop still goes into soft drinks worldwide, where it adds color and "pep" as well as an earthy flavor.

Medicinally, cola acts as a moderate central nervous system and heart stimulant, with an uplifting quality that makes it a wonderful antidepressant. Its stimulant effect is balanced by its earthy, grounding, and strengthening nature.

It has a traditional use in staving off fatigue, hunger, and thirst (much like coca in South America), with a feel-good settling of the stomach and stressed or worried minds. As such it promotes the appetite in all senses and enhances bodily energy and awareness.

Cola has a low-key reputation as an aphrodisiac, but we rate it highly for taste, uplift, and invigoration.

COLA COFFEE

Cola combines really well with coffee, adding an earthy depth. Add a teaspoon of **cola powder** to enough **coffee** for two people. Brew as normal. A little cinnamon, a few pods of cardamom, or a piece of vanilla bean can also be ground with the beans for added flavor and aphrodisiac effect.

COLA DECOCTION

Put 2 cups **water** and 1 tablespoon **cola powder into a saucepan.**

Bring to a boil. Turn down heat. Cover and simmer gently for 10 minutes.

Strain through a cloth when cool.

Add 2 tablespoons per cup of **apple juice** or **sparkling apple** or **white grape juice.**

Real Cola

4 cups **water**
2 tablespoons **cola powder**
1 cup **sugar**
juice of half a **lemon**
¼ teaspoon **vanilla extract**
sparkling water

Bring first two ingredients to a boil. Turn down heat. Cover and simmer gently for 10 minutes.

Strain through a cloth.

Pour back into a clean saucepan. Add **sugar.** Boil for about 5 minutes.

Cool.

Add **lemon juice** and **vanilla extract.**

Add **sparkling water** to taste.

DAMIANA

Damiana is a superb tonic for both sexes. It is a pleasant-tasting herb that can be simply taken as a tea or incorporated into more exotic recipes, though some people prefer to call it a "nervine," or nerve tonic, rather than an aphrodisiac.

The herbal literature is undecided whether damiana is an aphrodisiac, because few human clinical trials have yet addressed the issue. This academic doubt is recent, as previous generations, and medical officialdom, were happy to name this plant after the sixteenth-century herbal pioneer William Turner, and acknowledge its main use, as *Turnera aphrodisiaca*. The famous British herbalist, Mrs. (Maud) Grieve, writing in 1931, still used this name, but modern science specifies *Turnera diffusa* as opposed to *aphrodisiaca*.

Incidentally, the common name damiana has even more distinguished origins, being a tribute to Saint Damian (martyred in AD 303), the patron saint of pharmacists.

The ancient Mayans of Central America used damiana as an aphrodisiac. Most Mexicans today have no problem in regarding damiana as a direct

Damiana, *Turnera diffusa*, is a Central American plant with pretty yellow flowers. It is harvested while flowering, so the dried herb will be composed of leaves, stems, and flowers.

Also used for depression, anxiety, spasms, urinary complaints, diabetes, and menstrual problems.

Warming and drying.

- tonic
- increases libido
- calming
- hormone balancing

Avoid during pregnancy. May reduce blood sugar levels, so exercise caution if you have hypoglycemia.

sexual stimulant and antidepressant for both sexes. It is also the main ingredient of a popular alcoholic cordial, sold in bottles the shape of a woman's torso, in Mexico and the United States.

Damiana has a pleasant taste, aromatic and slightly sweet, that is refreshing as a simple tea or that can be adapted well to more exotic recipes. We find it mixes well with licorice and rose, a combination that enhances its restorative and hormone-balancing properties. It is also a good addition to chilis and garlic in savory dishes.

You will feel the most benefit from damiana with regular use as a daily nerve and hormonal tonic, which builds its full effect over several weeks.

Mexicans, old and young, believe that damiana is an effective and safe aphrodisiac.

DAMIANA BUTTER SAUCE

Melt 1.75 oz. **butter.** Add 1 heaping teaspoon **dried damiana** and infuse for about 10 minutes. Dried damiana is often a bit woody, so strain the melted butter into a clean dish, then add 1 **clove crushed garlic** and about 1 teaspoon **crushed green chili,** or to taste.

Dip artichoke leaves or freshly steamed asparagus in it, or serve over your favorite aphrodisiac dish.

ROSE & DAMIANA ELIXIR

Fill a jar half full with fragrant **rose petals.** Add 3 tablespoons **dried damiana,** a tablespoon each of **ashwagandha** and **shatavari root** (optional), and a stick of **cinnamon.** Fill to half or three-quarters full with **brandy** or vodka and fill the rest of the way with **honey.** Leave for 4 to 6 weeks, shaking or stirring occasionally, then strain and bottle. Have a liqueur glassful as desired.

Damiana & Licorice Tea

Mix roughly equal parts of dried **damiana** and dried **licorice root**. If you like a sweeter tea, use more licorice.

Use a heaping teaspoonful per cup of **boiling water**. Cover and steep for about 5 minutes. Strain and drink.

Damiana Iced Tea

Mix 2 heaping teaspoons **damiana**, 1 heaping teaspoon **mint**, and some **rose petals**. Pour boiling **water** on them and brew for 5 minutes. Strain and chill. Serve over ice.

FIGS

Figs are succulently suggestive of sex and fecundity.

Figs may have been the real "apple" in the Garden of Eden, as fig leaves were the modest coverings for Adam and Eve after they ate the forbidden fruit. Some see ripe figs as male in shape and, when cut, exposing the multiple seeds encased in pulpy flesh, as female and fertile; others say the opposite. The favorite fruit of Cleopatra, it has been used as an aphrodisiac wherever it is grown—forbidden or not!

D. H. Lawrence's 1923 poem "Figs," excerpted here, comes closer than most to the heart of its (and his) sexuality.

> *Fig, fruit of the female mystery, covert and inward,*
> *Mediterranean fruit, with your covert nakedness,*
> *Where everything happens invisible, flowering and*
> *fertilisation, and fruiting*
> *In the inwardness of your you, that eye will never see*
> *Till it's finished, and you're over-ripe, and you burst to*
> *give up your ghost.*

Although wonderful used in roast dishes as a glaze, figs are irresistible when fresh and ripe. Pick from the tree on a hot day (steal the figs from the

Figs are the fruit of a small tree, *Ficus carica*, native to Persia and the Mediterranean.

The best way to have fresh figs is to grow your own, if you live in the South or West. They are a special treat for a brief period in summer, so don't be stingy!

● sweet and succulent

wasps if necessary), or gently heat seasonally bought figs in the oven. The rich, creamy filling of our recipe contrasts the sweetness of orange juice and licorice with the spicy tang of black pepper.

While dried figs can be soaked and warmed, they don't look or taste as good as the real thing. Make the most of figs' ripeness in season!

STUFFED FIGS

Mix in a small bowl:

> 1.75 oz. **cream cheese**
> ½ tablespoon **orange blossom water**
> ½ tablespoon **epimedium tincture**
> ½ teaspoon **licorice root powder**
> ¼ teaspoon freshly ground **black pepper**

Select 2 ripe fresh figs. Make two slices in each fig from the top, almost to the bottom, to create an X. Spoon or pipe the mixture into the center of each fig, squeezing the sides together gently. Chill them until you are ready to eat them.

GINGER

Ginger is equally a spice, a food, a drink, and a medicine. Its characteristic is heat: warming to hot in the fresh rhizomes and hot to very hot when dried into powder.

Ginger root, Jamaica ginger, *Zingiber officinale*

Tropical, grown from South America (Brazil is the major producer) to India, China, and Southeast Asia. Underground rhizomes are used medicinally; flowers can be eaten.

Use fresh ginger or the dried powder.

One Ayurvedic writer describes ginger as "the herbalist's best friend," an anti-inflammatory and antibacterial, used for flu, fevers and colds, nausea, diarrhea, raising "digestive fire," and inducing sweating.

● stimulant

Ayurveda in India and traditional Chinese medicine recognize different uses for fresh and dried ginger, and have given them different names. In Western terms, fresh ginger gently increases peripheral blood circulation, including to the genital areas, and lowers blood pressure; dry ginger is stimulating from the heart outwards and is more used to treat cardiac conditions and for its blood-thinning properties.

On this basis, fresh ginger is more directly aphrodisiac, though both forms are used wherever ginger grows or is marketed. It can be grated over savory or sweet food and taken as a tea (with honey) indefinitely and safely, with pleasure and without ill side effects.

Research has shown that atherosclerosis (clogging) of the penile artery is the cause of half the cases of erectile dysfunction in men over fifty. Ginger, garlic, and chilis are among the foods that can reverse or reduce this depressing statistic and deserve to be thought of as daily aphrodisiac aids.

Ginger Grenadine

Pour the juice of a **lemon** and a cup of **apple juice** into two tall glasses; top up with real **ginger ale**. Add **ice**. Slowly pour in **grenadine** to create shades of light and dark in the glass.

Hot Ginger Sauce

Grate 1 piece **ginger**, about 1 ½ inches long. Crush 2 cloves **garlic** and about a teaspoon fresh chili. Add a teaspoon of **galangal** powder if you have it. Fry these together gently for a few minutes in **coconut oil** or **toasted sesame seed oil**. Add a small cup of **coconut milk**, some chopped **basil** or **coriander leaves**, a little **soy sauce**, and the juice of a **lime** or half a **lemon**.

This is a delicious sauce for stir fries, steamed vegetables, or curries.

Green Masala

Grind up a small piece of fresh **ginger**, 1 or 2 cloves of **garlic**, 3 or 4 fresh **green chilis,** and a small bunch of **fresh coriander leaves (cilantro)** with a little **water** to make a paste.

Serve this masala as a condiment or incorporate in recipes—use your imagination.

GINSENG

Ginseng has an ancient reputation as an aphrodisiac and rejuvenating tonic. It invigorates and energizes mind and body, and improves sexual performance. The best ginseng roots, sometimes decades old, fetch very high prices.

Asian, Chinese, or Korean ginseng is the root of the *Panax ginseng,* while American ginseng is a closely related plant, *P. quinquefolium*. Both species are slow-growing woodland perennials. There are around sixteen other species in the Araliaceae genus worldwide.

Siberian ginseng (Eleuthero or wucha) is not ginseng but a related plant, *Eleutherococcus senticosus,* which grows into a spiny shrub.

Ginseng can cause increased blood pressure in some people, so use with caution if you suffer from this (although studies have also shown ginseng to lower blood pressure).

- adaptogen
- stimulant

The Chinese name for ginseng, *ren shen,* means "man root." Ginseng is a plant that conjures up the mysteries of Asia, but surprisingly, vast quantities of ginseng have been exported from North America to China since the early nineteenth century. The American form is similar to the Asian species, both as a plant and in its effects.

Ginseng invigorates the mind and the body, reducing fatigue and building vitality and endurance. It improves erectile function and increases male fertility, especially among the elderly. Normalizing immune function, it is used to treat a wide range of conditions. It is particularly useful for depletion caused by overwork, stress, or illness, and can be used by both sexes if energy levels are low.

Asian ginseng is one of the most studied herbs in the world, so there is plenty of modern evidence from human research to support the traditional claims.

Roots are usually harvested when the plant is five to twelve years old, which is one reason they are so expensive. As with any high-price herb, substitutions are often made, which means that commercial ginseng drinks probably contain too little root to be therapeutic.

Ginseng root is white when harvested. The red Asian root has undergone a process of curing that gives it the red color and makes it more heating and stimulating. Herbalists generally consider the American ginseng less heating than the Asian and more suited to women and younger people.

It is thought that ginseng increases nitric oxide levels in the penis, as does Viagra, thus promoting blood flow and subsequent erection. Ginseng is safer (and usually cheaper) than the drug and is more natural.

The easiest way to take ginseng is simply to chew on a few bits of the cut root. Initially the taste is a little bitter, but as you chew and the root dissolves in your mouth, it leaves a lingering and energizing sweetness.

You can make a really good-quality ginseng extract by using the tailings, or small side roots, which are much cheaper than the large roots. Pictured on page 36 is fresh ginseng root.

Dried white and red Chinese ginseng roots

GINSENG TINCTURE

Fill a jam jar with chopped **ginseng root** or tailings and cover with vodka. Store in a dark place. Every day for a month, shake the jar. After the month is up, strain and bottle. Take a teaspoonful or two a day in the autumn and winter, or whenever you need an extra boost. Try it in our Athol Brose recipe (see the "Oats" chapter), or add it to hot chocolate.

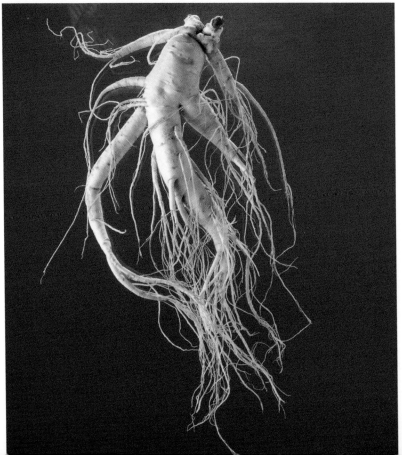

Ginseng & Schisandra Tea

Mix roughly equal parts **ginseng root, schisandra berry,** and **licorice root**. Add a tablespoon of the mix to 2 cups **water**, cover, and simmer gently for 10 minutes. Strain and drink either hot or chilled.

Ginseng Electuary

An electuary is a paste made of an herb and honey. Mix 2 tablespoons **ginseng powder,** 1 tablespoon **licorice powder,** and 1 teaspoon **cardamom powder** with enough runny **honey** to make a soft paste. This keeps quite well in a jar. Take a spoonful daily or for an occasional energy boost.

Asian ginseng

HORNY GOAT WEED

This ancient and reputable Chinese aphrodisiac has become hugely popular in Western health stores and on the Internet. Is this all hype, or does horny goat weed work as well as its name promises?

Horny goat weed was by far the most frequent ingredient in our straw poll of 100 Internet sites selling herbal aphrodisiacs and that also listed constituents (see part 2, "Other Aphrodisiacs"). It had hits in just over half of the sites sampled, with the next one, ginseng, registering a third.

Does this make horny goat weed the best current aphrodisiac—or is this hype, wishful thinking, placebo? The name is a marketing dream, but this translation of yin yang huo is not the only one: The leading book in English on Chinese herbal medicine renders it "licentious goat wort." Would that have hit the jackpot, too?

The name is from the tale of a Chinese goatherd who found that his goats (or, in some versions, a monster called yin yang) became sexually insatiable when eating the leaves of a low-growing plant. Incidentally, you may have horny goat weed growing in your garden as Epimedium, an attractive perennial ground cover.

This is a reputable kidney and liver tonic, and it needs time to work through and tonify your whole system. Take daily as a tea, liqueur, or tonic formula for, say, four to six weeks. Just don't expect immediate results. It is proven to increase sperm count and harden erections, and is a libido enhancer in women, so the effect is worth waiting for.

HORNY GOAT WEED TEA

Put 2 tablespoons of dried **horny goat weed leaves** in a teapot and pour in 2 mugfuls of **freshly boiled water.** Cover and let steep for about 5 minutes, then strain. Pour into two mugs. It has a slightly sweet taste that is warming and pleasant. Can be used cold in a cake icing.

HORNY GOAT WEED LIQUEUR

Loosely fill a large jar with dried **horny goat weed leaves.**

Add: a slice or two of **orange**
        3 or 4 **cardamom pods**
        1 tablespoon **brown sugar**

Pour in enough **whiskey** to fill the jar and submerge the contents. Put the jar in a warm dark place for two weeks, then strain and bottle.

Enjoy a small liqueur glassful, sipped slowly.

TONIC APHRODISIAC FORMULA

This is a formula made from herbal tinctures, but it can easily be adapted to powdered dry herbs in the same proportions.

Mix 6 parts **Epimedium,** 5 parts **damiana,** 5 parts **ashwagandha,** 4 parts **muira puama,** 3 parts **saw palmetto,** and 2 parts **licorice** tinctures. (Each part can be taken as 10 ml, a teaspoon, or any measurement of your choice.)

Dose: 1 teaspoonful three times a day.

JASMINE

The fragrance of jasmine is euphoric, heady, and sensuous—smelling the flowers or dabbing the oil (absolute) on the tip of your nose is blissful. Jasmine has always been associated with love and weddings. It is prized by perfumers for the way it combines muskily masculine and florally feminine qualities, the sensuous and the spiritual.

Jasmine's aphrodisiac qualities are related to its fragrance, and any of the fragrant species can be used. *Jasminum officinale* is the hardiest, while *J. grandiflorum* is most often used for perfume and *J. sambac* is generally used to flavor teas.

In Hindu folklore, the god of love anointed his arrow tips with jasmine oil before piercing the hearts of lovers. Jasmine was used by lovers in ancient Persia to perfume their bodies, and in Sufi poetry jasmine is a symbol of divine love and longing for spiritual union.

Jasmine is unique in the way it encompasses apparent opposites. It is both muskily masculine and florally feminine. It is earthy and enlightening, sensuous and spiritual, yin and yang. It has been associated with the moon and with Jupiter, and has been called both "king of perfumes" and "queen of perfumes." It is considered by some to be warming and by others to be cooling, and is used in fragrances for both men and women.

Emerging into full glory after sunset, jasmine is the fragrance of warm, steamy nights. It is euphoric, rich, heady, and sensuous. The scent of jasmine instantly makes you feel happier. If you have a garden, plant jasmine and strew fresh jasmine flowers over your pillows, where they will release their perfume all night long.

We were in central Cyprus a few years ago, renting a house in an orange orchard. All day long the scent of orange flowers permeated the air. At night, though, a single jasmine plant overwhelmed every other scent. It was exactly as Keats wrote in "Endymion," a lover's poem if ever there was one:

> *It was a jasmine bower, all bestrown*
> *With golden moss. His every sense had grown*
> *Ethereal for pleasure.*

Jasmine flowers are edible and will add a sensuous flavor to tempt the palate. Their slight edge of bitterness balances the sweetness of their scent.

Jasmine is heat sensitive, and the essential oil cannot be extracted with steam, as it can be for most flowers. The perfume was traditionally made by enfleurage, a lengthy process that layers the flowers on top of a cold purified fat, and then extracts the scent in alcohol. It is very labor intensive, hence costly.

Today, most jasmine oil (absolute) is extracted chemically with solvents. It is still very expensive: Eight thousand jasmine flowers yield only one gram (or 0.0352739619 ounce) of absolute. Use jasmine absolute as a perfume, alone, or mixed with other heady scents, and as a sensuous addition to massage oils.

JASMINE OIL

You can make your own natural jasmine oil easily at home if you have a flowering vine.

Melt a thin layer of **coconut oil** on a nonstick baking tray. Allow it to solidify at room temperature, then lay a layer of **fresh jasmine flowers** over it. This works best if the flowers are picked in the evening or early in the morning, when their scent is strongest. Cover the flowers with a sheet of wax paper.

Replace the flowers with fresh ones every couple of days. After a week or two, the oil should have a good scent of jasmine. It is not nearly as strong as an absolute, but it is made without solvents.

It can be used as a perfume and is a wonderful oil for the face or to massage the body.

Jasmine Fruit Salad

Put in a bowl together:

    ½ cup **cherries,** halved and pitted
    ½ cup **cape gooseberries,** halved
    ½ cup **green seedless grapes**
    1 tablespoon **jasmine flowers**

Mix well. Drizzle with **honey** or **cardamom syrup** (see the "Cardamom" chapter) and serve.

CRYSTALLIZED JASMINE FLOWERS

Put in a small jar:

>   2 tablespoons **rosewater**
>   1 ½ tablespoons **gum arabic**

Put the lid on and shake well. Leave overnight for the gum to fully dissolve.

Pick jasmine flowers, ideally in the early morning when their scent is strongest.

Use a fork to dip the flowers into the rosewater solution, then shake off the excess. (If you are doing a large batch, it works well to put the flowers on a saucer to drain while you dip more flowers.)

Lay each flower on **superfine sugar** in a small bowl, and sprinkle sugar over the flower so that it is thinly coated. Place the flower on a cookie sheet to dry. When you've finished dipping all the blossoms, place the cookie sheet in an open cupboard to dry for a few days. Once crisp, the flowers can be stored in an airtight container until you are ready to use them.

JASMINE TINCTURE WITH ICE CREAM

Choose a good **vanilla ice cream** or ice cream substitute. Scoop into two small bowls. Pour a teaspoon or two of **jasmine tincture** on top, and decorate with **crystallized jasmine flowers**.

JASMINE PUDDING

Put 1 tablespoon of **jasmine tea** in a small saucepan.

Pour in about ⅓ cup **boiling water,** and leave to infuse for 1 minute.

Add 2 level tablespoons **superfine sugar and** ½ cup **half-and-half.**

Slowly bring to a boil over low heat, stirring constantly. Check the taste until the cream is well flavored. Strain the cream into a clean saucepan.

Dissolve 1 teaspoonful **agar** in ½ tablespoon **water,** and add to the cream. Simmer gently until the agar has dissolved. Pour into two dessert dishes and chill until set. Decorate with fresh jasmine flowers, if available.

MACA

Maca is an unlikely candidate as an aphrodisiac: An unspectacular root crop grown high in the Andes, it resembles a turnip or swollen radish, but it has become an Internet sensation.

Maca, or Peruvian ginseng, is the tuber of the plant *Lepidium meyenii*, an Andean crop in the cabbage family. Use powder or tincture.

- tonic
- performance enhancing
- stimulant

Thriving high up where no other crops survive in poor soils and freezing, windswept weather, maca is a traditional source of nourishment for man and beast alike in the Peruvian mountains, where, to their surprise, the Spanish conquistadors found "well-fed babies and tall adults."

Local people attributed their health and fecundity to a diet of baked or boiled maca, which also helped the Spanish horses regain strength and fertility. Inca warriors were given maca to increase their martial ardor; after conquering a town, they were forbidden more maca, to protect the local women from their amorous attention.

Maca is often promoted as "Peruvian ginseng," though the two species have no botanical relationship. They do reportedly share such medicinal benefits as metabolic and mental stimulation, steroidal hormone balancing, aiding recovery from fatigue, and libido enhancement for both sexes (notably for men with erectile dysfunction and women at menopause). So great is the Internet interest in maca and its enthusiastic hyping that its sustainability as a Peruvian export crop is under threat.

Maca is thought to be so aphrodisiac because of high amino acid levels. Research highlights two: Maca's arginine helps produce nitric oxide, which increases sperm production and activity, and its histidine assists successful ejaculation. Maca does not add testosterone, contrary to the claims of some websites.

Maca is a staple food, remember, and its benefits are cumulative over long periods; it is not an instant drug. The powder smells like butterscotch, but it's blander and slightly bitter. Drinking maca powder stirred into fruit juice or water makes the scalp tingle. Add it to porridge, breads, and cakes, and see why the Andeans enjoy it.

Maca Cupcakes

Warm together: ½ tablespoon **cider vinegar**
1 tablespoon **dark corn syrup**
4 tablespoons **butter**
½ cup **light brown sugar**

When soft, beat until creamy.

Add: ½ cup **milk** or **oat milk**
1 cup **all-purpose flour**
2 tablespoons **maca powder**

Mix until well blended.

Pour 1 tablespoon **boiling water** over ½ teaspoon **baking soda** and stir into the cake batter.

Pour into a 10-muffin pan and bake at 350°F for 15 to 20 minutes, until golden on top and cooked through. Cool.

Alternative: Also delicious with 2 teaspoons ginger powder instead of the maca.

Vanilla Fudge Icing

Melt 1 teaspoon **butter** in a saucepan.

Add: 1 ½ cups **sugar**
½ cup **milk**
½ teaspoon **salt**

Stir until it reaches boiling point. Continue cooking until the mixture reaches the soft ball stage (240°F). Cool a little, then add ½ teaspoon **vanilla extract** and beat until smooth. Spread on the cupcakes. If the icing gets too stiff, warm it over hot water. Decorate the top of each cupcake with a small, very ripe **strawberry** while the icing is still soft.

Matthew loves the combination of hard, sweet icing; a soft, light cake; and a luscious strawberry melting in the mouth, and we think you will, too.

MANGO

A ripe mango, especially warm from the sun, is a sensuous, succulent pleasure to eat. The rich flavors and smooth texture caress the mouth. How could such pleasure not be aphrodisiac?

Mangos are the fruit of a tall, long-lived tropical tree, *Mangifera indica*. There are many different varieties, each with their own unique characteristics (Alphonso is top rated in India), but we've yet to taste one that wasn't delectable.

● sweet and succulent

There is an episode of *Seinfeld* where Kramer gives George a piece of mango to try. George, forever skeptical, first just says it's juicy and ripe, then after a few seconds shouts out: "It's like a shot of B12—it's a taste explosion!" He goes for the biggest piece.

Our advice would be to follow George. Mango flesh in season has the color of sunshine and the ambrosia of honey. It is messy, deliciously so, and you are bound to get juice on your chin and strings in your teeth. You will probably gnaw the stone to extract every last taste. It doesn't matter; have another.

When it's summer and mango fever strikes, as we hope it will, the only practical thing to do—and this is our main mango recipe—is to eat it while naked, preferably in a hot bath, sharing—at least—the water with your loved one.

Mangos are good green, too, when the flesh is sourer and more acid. *Amchar* is mango powder that gives a tang to samosas, chutneys, and curries. The green fruit is drying, antibacterial, and rich in vitamin C, whereas the mature fruit has more vitamin A (sorry, George, not B12). Sweet mango goes into jams and a mild chutney, but as a fruit it is incomparable.

The taste of ripe yellow mango is hard to describe, but that doesn't deter all authors. E. J. Banfield made a worthy attempt in his 1911 memoir, *My Tropic Isle.* It's the book's centenary as we write:

Take of a pear all that is mellow, of a peach all that is luscious, of a strawberry all that is fragrant, of a plum all that is kindly, of an apricot all its aroma, of cream all its smoothness. Commingle with musk and honey, coriander and aniseed, smother with the scent of musk roses, blend with cider, and the mixture may convey a dim sense of some of the delectable qualities of one kind of mango.

HOW TO RIPEN YOUR MANGO

Put it in a brown paper bag, by itself or with an apple or banana. It's ready when it has a sweet aroma and the flesh gives a little on gentle pressing.

Slice down either side of the flat stone (the stone is at the widest part of the fruit), cut in cubes down to the skin, then turn the skin out to expose the flesh. Delicious just as is, or pour cardamom syrup (see the "Cardamom" chapter) or passion fruit pulp over the mango before devouring.

Mango with cardamom syrup

MUIRA PUAMA

This Amazonian tree is known as "potency wood," its bark and roots having a long-standing reputation as an aphrodisiac.

Ptychopetalum olacoides is a small Amazonian forest hardwood tree with jasminelike scented white flowers. It is the bark and root that are used.

There is some confusion because another Amazonian tree, *Liriosma ovata,* is also called muira puama.

The dried wood can be boiled to make a decoction, or use the powder or a tincture.

Muira puama is used as a tonic for the nervous system and is antidepressant. It is considered safe, with no reported drug interactions.

● stimulant

Muira puama is called "potency wood," referring to the local use of its powdered bark and roots as an aphrodisiac drink and tincture for both sexes. It is recognized as an aphrodisiac in Brazilian herbalism and has been used in a low-key way in Europe since at least the 1930s, though its reputation is currently gathering pace. Another Amazonian species, *Liriosma ovata,* is also called muira puama but has different medicinal effects.

Muira puama appears to be a safe, powerful aphrodisiac without reported side effects (apart from overstimulation leading to sleeplessness in some cases), toxicity, or drug/plant interactions—though as yet there have been few human clinical trials.

The plant's active constituents are not water soluble in heat, which means that even a long decoction will not extract them as effectively as an alcoholic tincture.

One European writer has suggested this recipe for a muira puama cocktail: Combine 5 tablespoons of muira puama powder with small amounts of star anise, galangal root, and cinnamon. Warm 3 cups of

vodka and add the herbs and spices. Bottle the mixture and put it aside for four days, then filter and serve.

Our recipe using muira puama tincture took quite a bit of processing to blend the dates and macadamia nuts, but it produced a tasty cheesecakelike tart.

MUIRA PUAMA AND DATE TART

Process into a smooth paste:

   3.5 fl. oz. **muira puama tincture**
   8 oz. chopped moist **dates**
   1 cup **macadamia nuts**

Grease an 8-inch springform pan.

Sprinkle 2 oz. **ground almonds** or macadamia nuts evenly over the bottom of the pan. Spread the date mixture over it.

Whip 1 ¼ cups whipping **cream** until stiff. Add 1 teaspoon **vanilla extract** and chill, preferably overnight or for at least an hour. Top the tart with the whipped cream mixture.

NUTMEG & MACE

These two spices were once worth more than gold. Their price and exotic rarity increased their aphrodisiac reputation, but they do work.

We were in south India on a tour of a spice garden. As we stopped by a nutmeg tree, our guide, Krishna, told us about a friend's wedding day. The groom had heard that mace was an aphrodisiac and even stronger than nutmeg, so he made sure he had lots of it. But instead of an amorous honeymoon, he fell sound asleep for three days.

What the man hadn't been told is that nutmeg and mace are dose dependent. While a little will reliably boost the libido and enhance the performance, a larger amount is narcotic and conducive to sleep—Julie uses nutmeg in capsules for sleep problems.

Opening a nutmeg fruit is a sensuous experience in itself. The outer pulp is pale and fleshy, but within that comes a splash of wet, moist, and lacy red fibers, the mace. This conveys nutrients to the nut, like fingers enfolding it. Sadly, like much beauty, mace fades quickly and soon dries to a dull orange.

A bag of nutmeg we bought in Zanzibar bore this somewhat enigmatic advice: "This is better for

drinks, cooking and for woman that given up strong desire for making or to fulfill their men. You have to break and inside you get nut that what we used for cooking like meat etc." Clear?

Nutmeg Nog

Heat 2 cups of **milk** or **almond milk** with a few squares of **white chocolate**, ½ teaspoon **nutmeg powder**, and ¼ teaspoon **vanilla extract**, stirring until almost boiling. Pour into cups and sprinkle a little nutmeg powder on top.

Mini Mace Cheesecakes

Mix together until smooth:

> 7 oz. **cream cheese**, warmed to room temperature
> 1 tablespoon **icing sugar (confectioners' sugar)**
> ½ teaspoon **mace powder**
> ¼ teaspoon **vanilla extract**

Spread the mixture evenly onto 4 **ginger snaps**, using a knife or your finger to smooth the edges and tops. Chill for an hour or two before serving. (Don't leave too long, or the cookie base may become too soft.)

NUTS & SEEDS

NUTRITIOUS NUTS:
almond, brazil, cashew, chestnut, coconut, ginkgo, hazel, hickory, macadamia, pecan, pine, pistachio, walnut

SUPPORTIVE SEEDS:
linseed, mustard, pumpkin, sesame, sunflower

Nuts and seeds are the reproductive vehicles of plants and trees, full of the DNA and nutrition the seedling needs. Highly concentrated foods and snacks (e.g., salted peanuts), they are also made into massage and eating oils (e.g., almond, sesame, sunflower, walnut) and other foods (e.g., halva and tahini from sesame, milk from almonds, puree from chestnuts).

Some seeds have specific aphrodisiac profiles. **Pine nuts** contain testosterone and are a male aphrodisiac in cultures from Europe and Arabia to Asia. Galen, the Greek physician to Roman emperor Marcus Aurelius, said a mixture of honey, almonds, and pine nuts, eaten on three consecutive evenings, produces a surge in male vitality. Pine nuts make a good aphrodisiac garnish.

Pumpkin seeds are renowned for their high zinc content, which is needed for healthy sperm, and are a much cheaper alternative to oysters. The seeds are often used for treating prostate problems. **Sesame seeds** are known to promote breast milk in nursing mothers.

Freshly shelled nuts offer the best flavor. Soaking nuts and seeds overnight before eating helps unlock their nutrition. Alternatively, dry roasting them briefly in a frying pan will bring out the flavor and make grinding them easier. Use the ground form within two days for best results, and do not store for long periods.

Stuffed Apricots

This recipe combines the aphrodisiac qualities of almonds with plump, succulent apricots. Peaches could also be used.

Mix together: 1.75 oz. **ground almonds**
2 tablespoons **maple syrup**
1 teaspoon **orange flower water**

Divide the almond paste into four portions, and roll each into a rough ball.

Take 4 **large apricots,** and slice each carefully down the crease on one side and remove the pit. Place a ball of almond paste in each one and squeeze gently closed.

Bake at 350°F for 15 minutes or until the almond paste is browning a little. Can be served with cardamom syrup (see the "Cardamom" chapter).

Gomasio

Gomasio, or Japanese sesame salt, is a condiment made from 5 parts **black sesame seeds** (these have an earthier flavor than the white seeds) to 2 parts **sea salt.** Dry roast the seeds, cool, and grind up together with the salt.

OATS

Oats have been cultivated for at least three thousand years. But the wildness is still there, in "green" oats or in the creaminess of the dried version—oats are still an old smoothie.

The grain we call oats is the seeds of a grass, *Avena sativa.*

Green milky oats are harvested before the seeds ripen, while oat straw and oatmeal are from the ripened plant.

Oats are a good tonic and reliable restorative for the nervous system.

● tonic

Oats have a sexy reputation. Lord Byron, for example, advised, "When young, sow wild oats; when old, grow sage." But what did he know? He was only 36 when he died. "Feeling your oats" can refer to both frolicsome horses and people. Seriously, though, is there evidence that oats can make you wild?

Green oats, collected from the brief "milky" stage of the seeds' development, are sold as an aphrodisiac. Human and animal studies show this form of oats will increase testosterone and act as a central nervous system restorative. Both green and dried oats make an excellent remedy for exhaustion, burnout, and fatigue, helping to reduce stress and allowing libido to revive.

Further, oats contain high levels of vitamin E, fiber, and polyunsaturated fatty acids. This has two positive consequences in terms of sexual health: Cholesterol levels in the blood can be lowered, and atherosclerosis (i.e., clogging of the blood vessels by fats) can be reduced. Freely flowing genital blood is vital for arousal in both sexes.

Oats are a nourishing food and drink—oat milk is silky smooth and sensual—that are best enjoyed long term and regularly. Indeed, porridge could be a medium for almost all the plants in this book!

Oats are also good in aphrodisiac combinations with damiana, ginseng, and saw palmetto, and are restorative on the skin and in the bath.

ATHOL BROSE

This is a traditional Scottish sweet that we have adapted for this book. Normally made with whiskey, it goes beautifully with herbal tinctures, in this case ginseng.

The recipe is much more delicious than it sounds! The bitterness of the ginseng disappears with the smoothing effect of the vanilla, and the cream and crunchy/chewy oats complement each other perfectly.

Toast 1 cup **rolled oats** in a cast iron or nonstick pan over medium heat until they are gently browned (do not allow to burn). Meanwhile, mix 2 tablespoons **runny honey**, 2 tablespoons **ginseng tincture**, and 1 teaspoonful **vanilla extract** in a bowl.

Whip 1 ¾ cups **heavy cream** or whipping cream until it feels light, and stir into the bowl. Add the crunchy oatmeal just before serving, folding gently into the cream mixture. Spoon into two tall glasses.

ORANGE

Orange blossom has long been associated with weddings, imparting its sweetness to the occasion. Bitter orange peel stimulates the appetite.

Bitter or Seville orange, *Citrus aurantium* var. *amara;* sweet orange, *Citrus aurantium* var. *dulcis.* A relative of other citrus fruits, including lemon, lime, mandarin, tangerine, satsuma, minneola, and grapefruit.

Parts used: bitter orange peel, bergamot oil (from bergamot oranges), leaves and twigs (as in petitgrain oil), flowers (as in neroli oil, orange flower water), whole fruit (as in Chinese medicine), and sweet orange fruit (juiced or eaten fresh)

- fragrant
- euphoric

Are oranges aphrodisiac? A morning glass of packaged orange juice isn't very sexy, but **neroli oil** certainly is. Neroli is the heady and expensive distilled oil of bitter orange flowers, emitting an uplifting, sensuous aroma that is also calming and counters depression. Use a few drops in the bath or as a massage oil with a carrier like almond oil.

Orange blossom water is the by-product of neroli distillation. It uplifts many cooked dishes and was Victorian ladies' standby for domestic emergencies yet mild enough for babies' colic. Buy it in Middle Eastern stores or online.

Eau de Cologne, the famous herbal water, took orange flower water to another level. The original eighteenth-century formula for this facial rinse combined bergamot orange oil, neroli, and rosemary leaves, distilled in grape juice. Good flower waters refresh your skin, and research shows they actually plump up the skin cells with nutrients, making it look and feel softer and younger.

In the **bitter orange** season (January), we made two aphrodisiac marmalades, adding yohimbe powder to one and muira puama to the other. Neither set properly (our fault for not using enough sugar), but both bore out John Evelyn's 1699 comments on bitter oranges: they "sharpen [the] Appetite . . . and impart an Aromatic exceedingly grateful to the Stomach."

MASSAGE OILS

Fragrance is an individual thing, depending on past memories and associations as much as on our actual sense of smell. Experiment to find combinations you like, but try these first if you're not sure where to start.

To a 1.75 oz. bottle of **sweet almond oil** or **camellia oil,** add 10 drops of **neroli essential oil.** Or try a combination of our favorite floral essential oils: 5 drops **neroli,** 2 drops **ylang-ylang,** 2 drops **jasmine,** and 3 drops **rose absolute.**

For a more earthy blend, take 1.75 oz. of **sweet almond oil** or **camellia oil** and add 1 drop **vetiver essential oil.** To a couple of teaspoons of this base oil, add 2 drops **petitgrain essential oil** and 2 drops **sandalwood essential oil.**

Orange flower water is used in our stuffed figs recipe; see the "Figs" chapter.

ROSE

Roses have long been a symbol of love. Their fragrance lifts the spirits and opens the heart. Roses are traditional gifts between lovers and are associated with beauty.

Roses are widely used as a flavoring in foods in the Middle East. Turkish delight, puddings, and cakes are often fragranced with rosewater, and fresh rose petals can also be used in a variety of ways. Egyptian apothecaries added them to skin preparations.

Roses and chocolates given to a lover on Valentine's, or any other day, are the most powerful symbols of love our culture has.

In Christian mythology, roses were always symbols of divine love. White roses particularly denoted purity. In the language of flowers, red roses were for passion, white for purity, and yellow for friendship.

Often thought of as a feminine flower, rose benefits men as well as women, helping balance hormones and emotions. Rose treats the heart on many levels, from the physical to the emotional. It is cooling, calming, and astringent.

In India, rose is used to increase libido, semen production, and fertility. It is also prescribed for gynecological problems, including excessive bleeding,

Rosa spp.
The best roses for aphrodisiac purposes are strongly fragrant deep red species.

Rosewater is a great skin toner, maintaining a healthy pH and moisture balance in the skin.

Rose preparations are astringent, antiviral, cooling, and help balance the hormones and emotions.

Use the fresh flowers, rosewater, rose tincture, or rose attar.

- fragrant
- increases libido
- hormone balancing
- relaxing

endometriosis, irregular periods, and fibroids. It calms the nerves and helps with depression, anxiety, and headaches.

Rose Cake

Beat until creamy: ½ tablespoon **cider vinegar**
1 tablespoon **dark corn syrup**
4 tablespoons melted **butter**
½ cup **light brown sugar**

Next stir in: ½ cup **milk**
1 teaspoon **rosewater**
1 cup **all-purpose flour**

Dissolve ½ teaspoon **baking soda** in 1 tablespoon **boiling water**.

Once dissolved, stir into the cake batter. Pour into two greased and floured 8-inch pans.

Bake at 350°F for 30 minutes or until done. Cool on a rack before removing cakes from the pans. Sandwich the two cakes with the rose filling and drizzle rose icing over the top (recipes follow).

ROSE FILLING

Blend until creamy:

>   handful chopped **rose petals**
>   4 oz. **butter, softened**
>   3.5 oz. **confectioners' sugar**
>   1 teaspoon **vanilla extract**

ROSE ICING

Slowly add 2 to 3 tablespoons **rosewater** to 1 cup **confectioners' sugar,** beating until the consistency of thick cream.

ROSE PETAL BATH

Run a warm bath and throw in a few handfuls of **fragrant rose petals**—or for a real extravagance, use enough rose petals to completely cover the surface of the water. Light some candles and enjoy a relaxing and uplifting bath.

You can also strew your pillows or the whole bed with fresh rose petals. It worked for Cleopatra (both in real and Hollywood versions).

ROSE MASSAGE

Rose attar or otto is a luxury as it takes about 30 roses to make just one drop. Use a few drops as a perfume, or mix a massage oil: Add 2 drops of **rose otto** to 2 tablespoons of **camellia** or **sweet almond oil.** Use to massage your partner or yourself, or add a little in the bath. Particularly effective when rubbed over the heart.

SCHISANDRA

Intensely flavored schisandra berries have been used as a tonic and aphrodisiac in China for at least two thousand years.

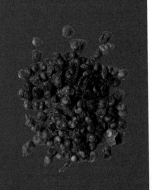

Schisandra is the fruit of a vine native to China, *Schisandra chinensis*, in the magnolia family.

Schisandra is also used to enhance memory and concentration.

Use the dried berry, powder, or tincture.

- tonic
- adaptogen

Schisandra has been revered medicinally in East Asia for thousands of years, being first described in writing in the later Han dynasty (first two centuries AD). Plants were brought to Western botanic gardens in the 1850s, and as an adaptogenic herb it has become increasingly popular in the West since the 1990s.

Its Chinese name means "five-flavor fruit," and you can test it for yourself with a schisandra tea made from the dried berries. Over a couple of minutes the taste intriguingly develops through acrid, sour, sweet, bitter, and salty—see how the sequence goes for you. We like to add licorice to bump up the sweetness and use the cooled tea for a wonderfully complex sangria or sorbet.

Schisandra is a famous Chinese sexual tonic used by both sexes to help regulate bodily secretions, as in reducing night sweats, premature ejaculation, and vaginal discharges. It is an effective nervous system stimulant and promoter of libido, but as an adaptogen it also works to soothe insomnia and as an antidepressant. It is taken in China for endurance and stamina in the bedroom as well as relieving stress. We recommend it as a subtle, safe, fascinating, and not so inscrutable experiment.

SCHISANDRA SYRUP

Add together in a saucepan:

> 1 cup **schisandra berries**
> 3 cups **water**

Cover and simmer gently for 30 to 40 minutes. When almost cool, put in a blender and blend for a few moments.

Strain through a sieve.

Return mixture to saucepan. Add 1 cup **sugar** and bring to a boil, cooking for a couple of minutes longer.

SCHISANDRA SORBET

Peel and slice a **banana** and freeze it. Also freeze 1 cup **schisandra syrup** mixed with the juice of 2 or 3 **oranges**. When frozen or nearly frozen, add the banana to the schisandra mixture and beat with a hand blender until smooth, then freeze again. Serve in a chilled dish.

SCHISANDRA SANGRIA

Empty a bottle of **red wine** into a jug. Cut an **orange**, a **lemon**, and a **lime** into wedges. Squeeze into the wine, then put the wedges in, too.

Add 1 cup **schisandra syrup**.

Chill overnight.

Add 1 cup sliced **strawberries** and about 4 cups of **ginger ale** just before serving.

SHATAVARI

Shatavari is the Ayurvedic name for wild asparagus root. Asparagus shoots are a modest aphrodisiac in Western tradition, but the Indian species has the more intriguing meaning of "the woman with a hundred husbands."

First question: How do we decode the name? Shatavari is a female (and male) aphrodisiac, but this is best understood within a context of the care and nurturing that this herb—or many men—might give to a loved woman throughout her life.

The generalization is often made that shatavari is the leading Ayurvedic herb for the female reproductive system, as ashwagandha is for the male, although both are beneficial for each gender. Is it not remarkable that shatavari is a proven tonic for each of the female reproductive life stages of menstruation, conception, pregnancy, birth, lactation, and menopause?

It achieves this breadth of action on the reproductive system by being a superb hormone and phytoestrogen balancer and rejuvenator. It is often called an adaptogen, a so-called intelligent herb that naturally and safely harmonizes the endocrine system.

Shatavari is the root of *Asparagus racemosus*, a wild asparagus native to India. It is a spiny vine that can clamber 30 feet or more up into the treetops.

Shatavari root can be boiled in water to make a decoction, or you can use the powder or tincture.

- hormone balancing
- adaptogen

Based on this understanding, shatavari will normalize irregular periods, increase milk flow, and reduce the heat of menopause. It will also heighten libido in both sexes and improve the quality of men's sperm, when the circumstances are arousing.

Shatavari is a green, thorny vine that grows throughout tropical Asia. In China the roots of the equivalent asparagus, *Asparagus cochinchinensis*, known as Tian men dong, are used to nourish the lungs and kidneys, and as a female hormone tonic.

In Indian and Nepali tradition, the roots are boiled with water or milk, clarified butter (ghee), and digestive herbs to increase shatavari's tonic properties. One standard formulation, shatavari ghrita, is a paste made of shatavari juice, ghee, and milk, boiled together with sugar, honey, and long pepper (white pepper can be substituted); ginger may be added. The paste is taken in small daily doses.

In the West, shatavari is more usually available as chopped roots or as a powder, which can be infused and drunk as a tea or taken in tincture form. It is also an ingredient in the famous narayana massage oil, where its considerable anti-inflammatory qualities are utilized.

Shatavari Electuary

An electuary is a paste made of an herb and honey. Mix shatavari powder with enough runny honey to produce a stiff paste. This can be stored in a jar and keeps for several months. Take a teaspoonful once or twice a day.

Shatavari, Almond Milk & Saffron

Bring to boil and simmer for 7 or 8 minutes:

> 2 cups **almond milk (or cow's milk)**
> 2 teaspoons **shatavari powder**
> 3 or 4 **cardamom pods,** crushed

Add a pinch of **saffron** and continue to simmer for half a minute longer.

Strain and sweeten to taste with **brown sugar.** If you like, add a little **rosewater** before serving.

Woman's Formula

Julie uses variations of this formula in her practice for women with low libido and low energy.

Mix tinctures of:

> 3 oz. **shatavari**
> 1.5 oz. **rose**
> 1 oz. **orange blossom**
> 0.75 oz. **cola nut**
> 0.75 oz. **cocoa**
> 1 teaspoon **jasmine**

Store in a dark glass bottle. Take a teaspoonful three times a day.

TRIBULUS

Who would have thought that this weed with nasty burs would turn out to be an important aphrodisiac? Its pretty yellow flowers carpet the ground after desert rain. Tribulus is strongly rejuvenating and strengthening.

Tribulus terrestris is also known as *gokshura*, puncture vine, and land caltrops. It is native to Africa, southern Europe, and Asia.

Either the whole dried plant or just the seed pods are used, as a tea, tincture, or powder.

It is also used for the urinary tract, muscle building, and as an antidepressant.

● hormonal stimulant

Tribulus is a yellow-flowered, summer annual weed of the Old World, with a range stretching from southern Europe through South Asia, China, and parts of Africa. It has naturalized in the Americas and Australia, often in desert areas.

Its many names are colorful, including caltrops, devil's thorn, goat head, puncture vine, *gokshura* or "cow hoof" (India), and *bai ji li* or "terror of the earth" (China). The reference is to the spiny fruit pods, which are so arranged that one of the sharp spikes is always upwards. The spines are strong enough to puncture tires or pierce cows' hooves; they made a fearsome battlefield weapon both for the ancient Greeks and the Zulu warrior Shaka some two hundred years ago.

But tribulus has another reputation, especially in traditional Indian medicine, and in the modern West, as an aphrodisiac. It is nourishing and rejuvenating to the reproductive system of both genders, with its saponins and flavonoids acting as hormone precursors. It appears that the protodioscin in tribulus is readily converted to a form of testosterone (DHEA), with sexually stimulating effects.

Raising testosterone levels has the associated effect of improving muscle building and stamina, and tribulus has been widely adopted by bodybuilders, especially in Bulgaria. Tribulus is also diuretic, and as a tea promotes urine where there is overretention; it has been used for prostate problems.

In India tribulus is often combined with ashwagandha for males and with rose and shatavari for females. Our panel tried a tribulus tincture. One male (fifty-five) said: "pleasant taste, strong arousal; lovely feeling with no irritation, and stimulation in a nice way." A female (forty-four) reported: "great— it's not your usual aphrodisiac; I need to retest it."

Tribulus is generally safe, though some users report an upset stomach. Check with an herbalist or doctor before using if you are taking antidepressants.

TRIBULUS BALLS

Grind ½ cup **sesame seeds** in an electric grinder.

Add 1 teaspoon **tribulus powder,** 1 teaspoon **cardamom powder,** ¼ teaspoon **cinnamon powder,** a pinch of **black pepper,** and ¼ cup **runny honey,** or enough to make a stiffish paste. Roll grape-size bits in whole **sesame seeds** to coat, then roll between your palms to make smooth balls. Chill until ready to eat. Makes about 20 balls, enough for several doses for two people.

VANILLA

The flavor of vanilla smooths and lifts recipes, both sweet and savory, to a new level. The rich fragrance is used in many perfumes, adding an erotic depth. Experiment with it for your own aphrodisiac recipes.

Vanilla is such a sexy orchid that its very name is derived from the Spanish for "little sheath," or vagina. A native of Mexico, it was an aphrodisiac for the Aztecs—Montezuma added it to chocolate in a foamy drink that reputedly helped him keep up with his fifty wives. Cortez and the conquistadors soon brought both products back to Europe, and a vanilla craze paralleled that for chocolate.

The centuries last passed have also given the taste important extension; the discovery of sugar, and its different preparations, of alcoholic liquors, of wine, ices, vanilla, tea and coffee, have given us flavors hitherto unknown.

—Jean Anthelme Brillat-Savarin (1755–1826)

Elizabeth I, it is thought, used vanilla to flavor her favorite almond sweet marchpane (marzipan), and Thomas Jefferson is said to be the first American to add vanilla to ice cream. He started something, as most vanilla today is produced synthetically for the US confectionery industry, including soft drinks; Coca-Cola, though, insists on "the real thing" and is the main user of vanilla extract.

The perfume industry rates vanilla highly, too. Perfumer Jean-Paul Guerlain says: "My grandfather Jacques taught me to like vanilla because it adds something wonderfully erotic to a perfume. It turns Shalimar into an outrageously low-cut dress."

Yet vanilla nearly denied itself all this fame and usefulness. When the vines were taken out of Mexico and grown elsewhere in the tropics, the plant usually flowered, but it would not pollinate and give seed pods. Only by curing fertilized pods can the active ingredient, vanillin, be released to give the unique taste and aroma we call vanilla. Another problem was that each vanilla flower lasts for only one day; if not pollinated, it will die.

For three centuries the botanical world could not work out why vanilla refused to reproduce outside Mexico. Then, in 1836, a Belgian scientist discovered that a membrane in the plant kept the male and female parts separate (so this aphrodisiac plant was self-contracepting), and that a specific small bee was needed to effect pollination. This bee, the Melipona, is only found in Mexico and would not relocate.

The answer came in 1841. An intuitive twelve-year-old slave boy on the French island of Bourbon (now Réunion), Edmond Albius, found that he could use a pointed bamboo stick to hold the membrane aside, and then with his thumb move pollen from the male to the female part. This geste d'Edmond technique is still used to pollinate vanilla today, and the Indian Ocean islands are the main producers. A good worker can fertilize two thousand vanilla flowers in a day.

Synthetic vanilla has been available since the 1870s, and the strangest things have been found to yield it, such as conifers, clovers, paper pulp, and even cow dung. **Vanilla extract** is a tincture of real vanilla pods, made with water and alcohol, and by law must contain 35 percent alcohol. **Vanilla essence** is distilled either from the extract, with added starch and sugar, or from an artificial source. **Vanilla powder** and **vanilla salt** are other commercial derivatives.

But the highest prices go to naturally cured **vanilla pods,** especially those with white vanillin crystals on the outside, known in France as "frost." The harvesting is laborious, as we noted, but so is the curing. Pollinated pods are left on the vine for up to nine months to ripen, picked by hand, immersed in hot water, and then slowly dried in the sun by day and rolled into blankets to "sweat" by night. Final curing, when the once green and odorless bean becomes black and scented, takes months more.

The best pods are black, slightly moist, pliable, and highly scented. Stored in an airtight tin, they can retain their aroma for 18 months. A good alternative is to keep one or two pods in a container of sugar, which means you will have vanilla-flavored sugar for cakes on hand as well as the vanilla itself. The pods can be recycled several times, although one of our favorite uses is to grind part of a pod to powder with our coffee beans.

COEUR À LA CRÈME

Coeur à la crème is a traditional French recipe made in small molds that are perforated and heart shaped. They can be bought in kitchen shops or online. If you don't have molds, simply drain the cheese in a lined sieve and shape by hand. Otherwise, line the molds with damp cheesecloth and let the cream cheese come to room temperature before starting. There are many different versions of this delectable dessert.

Beat together:

> 9 oz. package **cream cheese** (pour off any liquid first)
> ½ cup **crème fraîche** or **ricotta cheese**
> 4 tablespoons **confectioners' sugar**
> ½ teaspoon grated **lemon zest**
> seeds scraped from the inside of a **vanilla bean**

Press into the lined molds and chill overnight. To serve, turn the hearts out onto a plate and drizzle with **passion fruit,** as shown, or add your favorite strawberry or raspberry sauce, or fresh berries in season.

YLANG-YLANG

In Malay, ylang-ylang means "flower of flowers." The yellow-green blossoms have a rich, sensuous fragrance, and their oil is used in many aphrodisiac blends and high-quality perfumes. The effect is euphoric and languorous. It is a scent that makes you smile.

Ylang-ylang flowers come from a tropical tree, *Cananga odorata,* native to Malaysia and the Philippines.

Ylang-ylang is also a tonic for the nervous system and is deeply relaxing. It is euphoric and antidepressant. Used on the skin, it is cleansing for acne.

Use fresh flowers or essential oil.

● fragrant
● euphoric

Too much ylang-ylang essential oil can cause headaches and drowsiness. It's fine if you don't overdo it.

Ylang-ylang blossoms themselves look so relaxed that they seem about to drop off the branch. Their seductive scent evokes tropical heat and lethargy, removing tension while stimulating the senses.

If you are in the tropics, you can use fresh ylang-ylang flowers to scent a room, clothes, or your hair. The flowers were traditionally strewn on the beds of newlyweds in Indonesia.

In colder climes the essential oil is the usual way to buy ylang-ylang. A few drops can be added to coconut oil for a sensuous body massage; this mix was prized in Victorian times as macassar oil, used as a male hair conditioner.

The best form to buy is steam distilled and is known as ylang-ylang "extra." This is taken from the first distillation and is more costly, but it is well worth insisting on. What price euphoria?

BATH TRUFFLES

Cocoa butter is a wonderful neutral carrier for aromatic oils and fragrances, with an uncanny quality of melting at precisely the same temperature as our body heat. This means the "truffles" will be solid at room temperature but melt readily in the bath.

One aromatic bath truffle dissolved in your bath will make your skin feel soft and velvety, while the ylang-ylang is absorbed effortlessly as you relax in the heat.

Melt 3 oz. **cocoa butter** and add 20 to 30 drops of **ylang-ylang essential oil.**

Pour into heart-shaped chocolate molds or an ice cube tray.

Chill the molds in the fridge until firmly set, then remove the truffles. Store in a jar in a cool place.

To use, drop a truffle in a warm bath and allow it to melt. Be careful stepping in, as everything will become sensually slippery and slithery.

YOHIMBE

Yohimbe is among the top five aphrodisiacs for name recognition, along with (arguably) horny goat weed, ginseng, Spanish fly, and oysters. It is powerful, dangerously so in overdose, and we recommend using it with caution and respect.

Yohimbe is the bark of a West African tree, *Pausinystalia yohimbe* (*Corynanthe yohimbe* in older books).

Boil the bark as a decoction, or use powdered bark or tincture.

● stimulant

Yohimbe demands respect and caution in its use. Start with a little and see how it affects you before taking more. Avoid yohimbe if you have heart problems, high blood pressure, or suffer from migraine or panic attacks. Do not take if you are pregnant or breastfeeding.

Yohimbe is the local name for the bark of a large tree from tropical West Africa. Taken as yohimbe powder, and in its extract form, yohimbine hydrochloride, this is one of the best-known aphrodisiacs.

Until US law was changed in the 1980s, yohimbine, the extracted chemical, was the only Food and Drug Administration–approved over-the-counter "natural" aphrodisiac. Yohimbine is now a prescription-only drug for male sexual dysfunction in the United States, and in England is only available from registered pharmacists and approved professionals. Yohimbe the plant can be bought from herbalists, or as capsules in pharmacies and health stores. If you purchase online, you need to be sure that you are getting authentic, unadulterated yohimbe.

Yohimbe is still used in its source areas in celebration and ritual, with yohimbe tea being drunk before ceremonies with drums, fires, and dancing, followed by vigorous coupling. Yohimbe is a central nervous system stimulant and in larger quantities is mildly hallucinogenic, so if it's wild dancing and ecstatic sexual experience you seek, it could be the aphrodisiac for you.

You should be aware that yohimbe is dose dependent: Too low a dose for your personal physiology and psychology, and little happens; too much in your specific circumstances can cause unpleasant side effects such as raised blood pressure, heart palpitations, nausea, insomnia, and uneasiness. Both yohimbe and yohimbine should be avoided if you have a history of coronary heart disease, stroke, high blood pressure, migraine, or panic attacks, or if you are pregnant or nursing. If in any doubt, ask your doctor or an herbalist before you take yohimbe/yohimbine.

At the right dosage, the extract yohimbine (little research has been done on yohimbe as such) has been found in human and animal studies to increase frequency of sexual activity and to heighten sexual arousal; yohimbine also counteracts the turnoff feeling left by many antidepressants. Expect skin tingling and shivers down your spine, expanded awareness, and the feeling of blood flow to your genital area within a few minutes of taking the right dosage, and the effects will last up to about four hours.

Yohimbe has its risks, as we hope we have made clear. At the same time (and unusual among familiar aphrodisiacs), it has a clinical track record for treating male sexual dysfunction and a long tradition of ritual sexualized use in its African setting.

Yohimbe bought for teas resembles dried leaf mulch—red-brown, dusty, and somewhat oily. Start with a teaspoon for a large cup of boiling water and brew for five minutes. Some people like to add a teaspoon of vitamin C to moderate the rather acrid taste.

You can also buy yohimbe in capsule and extract form, but you do know less about the quality, strength, and reliability of these processed products than when you can obtain the dried herb from a reputable supplier.

Yo Cake

Warm until soft:

- ½ tablespoon cider vinegar
- 1 tablespoon dark corn syrup
- 4 tablespoons butter
- ½ cup light brown sugar

Beat until creamy, then stir in:

- ½ cup milk
- 2 teaspoons ground ginger
- 1 teaspoon yohimbe powder
- 1 cup all-purpose flour

Dissolve ½ teaspoon baking soda in 1 tablespoon boiling water.

Once dissolved, stir into the cake batter.

Pour into two greased and floured 8-inch pans.

Bake at 350°F for half an hour.

PART 2

OTHER APHRODISIACS

In a short book we have had to be severely selective, but we did want to mention other significant aphrodisiacs in this second part. **Kava kava** is here but would have been in the main section if it hadn't been proscribed in England a few years back, depriving users temporarily of one of the best euphorics; **black pepper, ginkgo,** and **saw palmetto** were next in line for our main list had there been room.

We are including many other plants because they occur in aphrodisiac formulas sold on the Internet, the way most people buy their aphrodisiacs. We feel it important to offer some explanation of what these plants are, even in this very brief form, so that buyers have more knowledge to inform their purchase.

To compile our list we surveyed one hundred current websites that fulfilled two conditions: first a listing in the top hundred or so hits for the search terms "herbal aphrodisiac" or "herbal Viagra," and, secondly, botanical constituents itemized. Both "male" and "female" interest sites were checked, and there was no control for place of origin, number of items in an aphrodisiac mixture, or type of herb. The criterion was popularity. Bear in mind that this was an informal survey and that things change rapidly in the virtual world. It is a snapshot of the most popular plant aphrodisiacs on the currently most popular buying medium.

We found **horny goat weed** to be the runaway leader with 52 citations in 100 formulas, followed by **panax ginseng** with 34; **damiana** and **ginkgo,** 31 each; **tribulus,** 28; **muira puama,** 27; the amino acid **L-arginine,** 26; **maca,** 25; **tongkat ali** and **yohimbe,** 21; and **saw palmetto,** 20. Also in our top twenty most popular online aphrodisiacs were **ashwagandha, catuaba, oats, rhodiola, schisandra, shatavari, Siberian ginseng, velvet bean,** and **wild yam.** We have covered all these along with others that scored at least two hits in our survey.

Listing is by common name in English where possible, but where the name used in commerce is in another language, that is preferred.

Agnus castus *(Vitex agnus castus).* Chaste Tree, Monk's Pepper. Leaves, berries make herbal tea or tincture; once thought to be aphrodisiac for women and anaphrodisiac for men, but effects vary with dosage.

Areca nut *(Areca catechu).* Seed of the tropical areca palm, also called betel nut. Usually rolled into betel leaf, making a mildly aphrodisiac stimulant favored in South and Southeast Asia.

Artichoke *(Cynara cardunculus).* A thistle from the Mediterranean. The boiled flower buds and heart of the globe artichoke are aphrodisiac in reputation—and what fun to eat!

Asparagus *(Asparagus officinalis).* The shoots, eaten as a vegetable, have a persistent aphrodisiac reputation. Culpeper (the famous herbalist Nicholas, 1653) wrote that the shoots "stirreth up bodily lust in man or woman."

Astragalus *(Astragalus membranaceus/propinquus).* Milk vetch, Huang qi. Root is an energizing tonic.

Ayahuasca *(Banisteriopsis caapi).* Caapi Yage. Amazonian vine used in ritual psychotropic beverages; vomiting often precedes "high."

Ba ji tian *(Morinda officinalis).* Morinda. A Chinese root used for impotence, infertility, and related problems.

Bala *(Sida cordifolia).* Country mallow. Native to India, it has high ephedrine content, making it stimulatory to the heart and genital blood flow.

Black cohosh *(Cimifuga racemosa, Actaea racemosa).* Black snakeroot. Root in Native American herbal lore treated multiple ailments; now used for PMT (premenstrual tension) and menopause treatments, and as a female aphrodisiac.

Brahmi *(Bacopa monnieri).* Water hyssop. Marshland succulent used in China and India as a sexual tonic.

Butea *(Butea superba).* Red kwao krua. Vine native to Thailand whose roots make a popular mild aphrodisiac locally; since the 1990s it's been sold online. Called a "miracle drug."

Calamus *(Acorus calamus).* Sweet flag. Roots of this wetland plant have been a popular tonic and aphrodisiac in China, India, and Egypt for millennia; banned since 1968 in the United States for use in food, though this is one strain only; three other strains are widely used medicinally.

Catuaba *(Erythroxylum vaccinifolium* or *Trichilia catigua).* Two rain forest plants with aphrodisiac reputations, both known as catuaba. In the state of Minas people say, "Until a father reaches sixty, the child is his; after that, the child is catuaba's." A love tonic.

Cistanche *(Cistanche deserticola)*. Rou cong rong. The fleshy stem of Chinese broomrape is aphrodisiac and a sexual tonic for both sexes.

Clavo huasca *(Tynanthus panurensis)*. Clove vine. Root and bark of a South American vine are aphrodisiac and stimulant; a key ingredient in local aphrodisiac rompe calzon, "bust your britches." Popular drink in the United States.

Coco de mer *(Lodoicea maldivica)*. Endangered palm from the Maldives, with a suggestively shaped nut; not used as an aphrodisiac.

Common curciligo *(Curculigo orchioides)*. Golden eye-grass, Xian mao. Rhizome of this Chinese plant is a sexual tonic.

Cordyceps *(Cordyceps sinensis)*. Caterpillar fungus, Dong chong xia cao (translated as "winter insect, summer grass"). Fruiting body of a Tibetan fungus that is parasitic on caterpillars; used as a sexual tonic.

Dodder *(Cuscuta epithymum)*. Cuscuta, Tu si zi. The seed of this Chinese parasitic plant is a sexual tonic.

Dong quai *(Angelica sinensis)*. Female ginseng. The root regulates menstruation and is a blood tonic.

Eleuthero *(Eleutherococcus senticosus)*. Siberian ginseng. This root was the first plant to be called an adaptogen, after much Soviet research; a sexual tonic.

Ferula *(Ferula hermonis)*. Zallouh, Lebanese Viagra. Resin and tincture of root long used as tonic and aphrodisiac in Mediterranean; found to stimulate estrogen and testosterone. Also mood elevating.

Galangal *(Alpinia galanga)*. Blue ginger, Kaempferia. Gingerlike rhizome called kah in Thai cuisine has similar warming and tonic effects to ginger.

Gardenia *(Gardenia jasminoides, G. augusta, G. taitensis)*. Zhi zi. The heavenly smell of the white flowers is perfect for weddings. In Tahiti it is mixed with coconut oil to make sensuous monoi de Tahiti, a superior bath truffle.

Garlic chives *(Allium tuberosum, Chinese leek)*. A warming seed used for sexual weakness.

Ginkgo *(Ginkgo biloba)*. Yin xing. Leaves of this ancient tree improve circulation, including in the brain (used for Alzheimer's). Taken as tincture, it helps erectile problems.

Gotu kola *(Centella asiatica/Hydrocotyle asiatica)*. Brahmi, Chi hsueh ts'ao. An adaptogen and circulatory stimulant; also for memory, tissue regeneration.

Guarana *(Paullinia cupana)*. South American vine with high caffeine content; more a heart tonic than aphrodisiac. Used for endurance. Brazilian national drink is guarana soda.

He shou wu *(Polygonum multiflorum)*. Fo ti, Chinese knotweed. Root is a rejuvenating tonic.

Honey (bee pollen and royal jelly). The oldest natural sweetener, long associated with sex (think honeymoon). Bee pollen is an energy superfood and libido enhancer, royal jelly a fertility-supporting antiviral. Mead and hydromel are alcoholic forms. So-called nectar of Aphrodite.

Iboga *(Tabernanthe iboga)*. Roots of a rain forest shrub from Central Africa. Small doses stimulate nervous system; larger doses are hallucinogenic.

Jequirity *(Abrus precatorius)*. Crab's eye, Ratti, Xiang si dou ("mutual love bean"). Red seed of a vetchlike tropical vine. Beautiful but poisonous—avoid!

Jujube *(Ziziphus ziziphus)*. Red date, Chinese date (or *Z. mauritiana*, Indian jujube). Fruit of small spiny tree; a calming, nourishing tonic.

Kava kava *(Piper methysticum)*. Vine related to pepper; root important in Pacific island cultures as ingredient of a relaxing and euphoric beverage.

Lycium *(Lycium chinensis)*. Wolfberry, matrimony vine. Is not a vine at all, but a rambling bush; berries are marketed as a tonic and superfood.

Nettle *(Urtica dioica)*. Seed is tonic and may be aphrodisiac; root helps prostate problems; leaves are highly nutritious. A wonder wild weed.

Palmarosa *(Cymbopogon martinii)*. Indian geranium, Rosha grass. Related to lemongrass and citronella; yields an aphrodisiac essential oil.

Passion fruit *(Passiflora edulis)*. Granadilla. Fruit of this tropical vine is delicious and full of seeds; good juice for aphrodisiac recipes.

Patchouli *(Pogostemon cablin)*. Leaves of tropical plant give the essential oil, famous in the 1960s, used in many perfumes; a grounding aphrodisiac.

Pepper *(Piper nigrum)*. Black pepper. Fruit of this tropical Indian vine is the familiar spice; stimulates appetite and circulation. Isabel Allende writes: "I go on record as saying that it brings joy to widows and alleviates the impotence of the timid."

Pomegranate *(Punica granatum)*. A small Mediterranean tree; red seeds and juice a famed tonic and aphrodisiac.

Prickly ash *(Xanthoxylum fraxineum [Zanthoxylum americanum])*. The bark tincture improves blood circulation.

Pumpkin *(Cucurbita maxima)*. Winter squash. Seeds a good source of zinc and essential fatty acids; beneficial for prostate and sperm health. Easy to find in shops and cheap, too.

Pygeum *(Pygeum africanum)*. Bark of this African tree is used for treating prostate problems.

Quebracho *(Aspidosperma quebracho-blanco)*. Bark of tree from northern Argentina. Contains yohimbine; aphrodisiac and mild antidepressant. Banned in some countries.

Rhodiola *(Rhodiola rosea)*. Golden root, rose root. Root of a plant from northern Europe and Asia; an adaptogen, which heightens memory, mood, and sexual performance.

Saffron *(Crocus sativus)*. The stigmas of this autumn-flowering crocus from Morocco, Greece, and Spain make the world's most expensive spice; antidepressant and mood uplifting.

Sandalwood *(Santalum album)*. A semi-parasitic tree that after growing thirty years gives divinely smelling essential oils; a calming aphrodisiac.

Sarsaparilla *(Smilax officinalis)*. Old US traditions of using this vine root for sexual dysfunction were confirmed by the 1939 discovery that it contains testosterone; use for limited periods.

Sassafras *(Sassafras albidum)*. A tonic and aphrodisiac tea is made from the roots; avoid the extracted safrole oil in large dosage.

Saw palmetto *(Serenoa repens)*. Berry of Carribbean palm. Sexual tonic; often used for prostate problems. Safe and adaptable, mixed with other tonics.

Skirret *(Sium sisarum)*. Crummock. Root vegetable in carrot family; considered "provoking unto venery" in old herbals. Tasty and easy to grow.

Suoyang *(Cynomorium songaricum, C. coccineum)*. Yang locker, Tarthuth. The fleshy stem of this Chinese, European, and Arabian parasitic plant is aphrodisiac and a sexual tonic.

Tongkat ali *(Eurycoma longifolia)*. Pasak bumi, Eurycoma. Small tree from Southeast Asia. Increases sexual desire and enhances performance and general well-being, but products on market are often adulterated. Endangered.

Truffles (the fungus). Have intense flavor and aroma, are incredibly costly, and strongly aphrodisiac. In France called "the testicle of the earth." An expression goes, "If a man is rich enough to eat many, slightly cooked under the embers, his loves will be many." Truffles in infused olive oil are more affordable.

Velvet bean *(Mucuna pruriens)*. Cowage, Nescafé, Kapikacchu. Legume, an aphrodisiac of ancient India, used for erectile problems. Contains L-dopa, and now treats Parkinson's.

Vetiver *(Chrysopogon zizanioides)*. Khus. Perennial grass native to India; roots yield an earthy, sensual essential oil.

Wild yam (*Dioscorea villosa*). American vine from whose root testosterone and progesterone are manufactured; the body cannot do this unaided, so beware claims of "natural" wild yam as a beneficial steroidal hormone.

ANAPHRODISIACS

In case some of the recipes we give are just too stimulating, you may need an anaphrodisiac, or libido buster. "Cold" plants like cucumber, lettuce, and wild lettuce have long been used in this way in Western herbal medicine, along with agnus castus, hops, dill seed, and rue. But do bear in mind Ovid's lament from two thousand years ago: "*Alas! There are no herbs to cure love.*"

Hops

HELPFUL SUPPLEMENTS

DHEA (5-dehydroepiandrosterone). An important sex hormone and precursor of testosterone; DHEAS is the sulfate (stored) form. Taken as a supplement to raise testosterone.

L-arginine, L-histidine, L-tyrosine. Three of the amino acids involved in the human sexual response, taken as supplements. L-arginine is converted to nitric oxide, increasing blood flow to the genitals; L-histidine activates histamine, involved in genital blood surges and orgasm; and L-tyrosine stimulates L-dopa in the brain to boost sexual desire.

Vitamin B complex. Among the B vitamins involved in sexual response are B5, in stamina; B12, in sperm production; niacin, in blood flow to the genitals; and choline, a neurotransmitter in sexual arousal.

Vitamin C. Research suggests low levels of vitamin C (ascorbic acid) lead to DNA damage in sperm, while supplementation or increased C through fresh fruit and vegetables improves sperm health and motility.

Zinc. An important element for production of testosterone and for preventing prostate problems; pine nuts, almonds, and pumpkin seeds are good sources, or use supplements.

Resources

RECOMMENDED SUPPLIERS

Frontier Natural Products Co-op, (800) 669-3275; www.frontiercoop.com. Offers a good range of organic herbs and spices, essential oils, etc.

Herbalist & Alchemist, (908) 689-9020; www.herbalist-alchemist.com. Mainly tinctures.

Horizon Herbs, (541) 846-6704; www.horizonherbs.com. Seeds and medicinal plants.

Starwest, (800) 800-4372; www.starwest-botanicals.com. Range of dried herbs, etc.

FINDING A PROFESSIONAL HERBALIST

Word of mouth is the best way to get recommendations—check with your friends. Complementary therapy clinics in your area may have herbalists working there, or you can ask in your local health food store. Lastly, to find qualified practitioners in your area, contact the American Herbalists Guild (AHG) (857-350-3128; www.americanherbalistsguild.com).

FURTHER READING

Allende, Isabel. *Aphrodite: A Memoir of the Senses.* London: Flamingo, 1999.

Buhner, Stephen Harrod. *The Natural Testosterone Plan: For Sexual Health and Energy.* Rochester, VT: Healing Arts Press, 2007.

Connell, Charles. *Aphrodisiacs in Your Garden.* London: Arthur Barker, 1965.

De Luca, Diana. *Botanica Erotica: Arousing Body, Mind and Spirit.* Rochester, VT: Healing Arts Press, 1998.

Hopkins, Martha, and Randall Lockridge. *InterCourses: An Aphrodisiac Cookbook.* 2nd ed. Waco, TX: Terrace Publishing, 2007. First edition published 1997.

Kilham, Chris. *Hot Plants: Nature's Proven Sex Boosters for Men and Women.* New York: St. Martin's Griffin, 2004.

Melville, Francis. *Love Potions & Charms: Over 50 Ways to Seduce, Bewitch, and Cherish Your Lover.* London: Simon & Schuster, 2001.

Rätsch, Christian. *Plants of Love: The History of Aphrodisiacs and a Guide to Their Identification and Use.* Berkeley, CA: Ten Speed Press, 1997.

Taylor, Leslie. *The Healing Power of Rainforest Herbs: A Guide to Understanding and Using Herbal Medicinals.* Garden City, NY: Square One Publishers, 2005.

Tisserand, Maggie. *Essential Oils for Lovers: A Sensual Guide to Aromatherapy.* London: HarperCollins, 1999.

Winston, David, and Steven Maimes. *Adaptogens: Herbs for Strength, Stamina, and Stress Relief.* Rochester, VT: Healing Arts Press, 2007.

Acknowledgments

This project has been ten years in the making, going through such possible formats as a cookbook or a reference text on the world's herbal aphrodisiacs. We are grateful to many people and gardens along the way, notably in Australia, Cyprus, India, Namibia, the USA, and Zanzibar. We owe particular thanks to our publishers, Merlin Unwin and Karen McCall, for believing in us and focusing us on a shorter but finally realizable practical guide to making your own aphrodisiacs.

Special thanks go to Janice and Ed Swab and Joe Hollis in North Carolina, Said Mohammed in Zanzibar, and Thomas Tomichen in Kerala for their kindness in helping us identify and photograph many of the plants featured in this book, and also to Jennifer Holland who got our damiana plant to flower in her greenhouse. All photographs are by Julie Bruton-Seal and in her copyright, unless otherwise noted.

Thanks to Christine Herbert and Karin Haile for checking the manuscript, and to a panel of friends who tested some of the recipes.

Index

About the Authors

Julie Bruton-Seal is a practicing medical herbalist and naturopath, photographer, author, and artist. She collaborated with her husband, Matthew ("my favorite author!"), on *Hedgerow Medicine* (2008; published in the United States as *Backyard Medicine*) and *Kitchen Medicine* (2010). They live in Norfolk, United Kingdom.

Matthew Seal is an editor, writer, and proofreader, and has worked on books, magazines, and newspapers in England and South Africa—"none has been as much fun as working with Julie."

Our website: www.hedgerowmedicine.com

Photo by Mary Plage